FAMOUS PHONIES

LEGENDS, FAKES, AND FRAUDS WHO CHANGED HISTORY

BRIANNA DUMONT

Sky Pony Press

NEW YORK

Sky Pony Press books may be purchased in bulk at special discounts for sales promotion, corporate gifts, fund-raising, or educational purposes. Special editions can also be created to specifications. For details, contact the Special Sales Department, Sky Pony Press, 307 West 36th Street, 11th Floor, New York, NY 10018 or info@skyhorsepublishing.com.

Sky Pony® is a registered trademark of Skyhorse Publishing, Inc.®, a Delaware corporation.

Visit our website at www.skyponypress.com.

10 9 8 7 6 5 4 3 2 1

Manufactured in China, July 2019
This product conforms to CPSIA 2008

Library of Congress Cataloging-in-Publication Data

DuMont, Brianna.
  Famous phonies : legends, fakes, and frauds who changed history / Brianna DuMont.
      pages cm – (The changed history series)
  Summary: "Famous Phonies: Legends, Fakes, and Frauds Who Changed History is the first in a new nonfiction middle grade series that will explore the underbelly of history, making you question everything you thought you knew about history's finest. It's perfect for the history buff, the reluctant reader, or that kid who loves the strange and unusual."—Provided by publisher.
  Audience: Ages 9-12.
  ISBN 978-1-62914-645-4 (hardback)
  1. Impostors and imposture—Biography—Juvenile literature. 2. Deception—Juvenile literature.
I. Title. II. Title: Legends, fakes, and phonies who changed history.
  CT9980.D87 2014
  920.02—dc23   2014022733

Cover design by Brian Peterson
Cover photo credit Wikimedia Commons Public Domain / Source: Clark Art Institute via
      Docu 2010
Interior illustrations by Bethany Straker

ISBN: 978-1-5107-5139-2
Ebook IBSN: 978-1-5107-5141-5

Contents

Author's Note

This book isn't about rewriting history. I don't want to obliterate anybody's beloved Bard. But this book is about *expanding* history. Let's leave it to the scholars in their ivory towers to debate the finer points of oral transmission in Ancient Greece, or how many ruffled Elizabethan actors it took to write a bawdy joke. It's their job to argue all day. My job is to bring those arguments down from the tower and give a new side to an old face. Taking the stuffiness out of those debates is just a bonus.

"History would be a wonderful thing, if only it were true." —Tolstoy

enter at your own risk

Introduction

Caution: Extremely Controversial

If you're looking for witty sayings by Confucius or electrifying tales of George Washington's brilliance, you've got the wrong book. Sure, those famous guys are in here, but it'd be dull as rocks to rehash stuff you've already learned. Besides, there's something those other books didn't tell you about these fabulously famous figures. They never existed.

Ah, got your attention, did I?

It's not as easy as all that, of course. Your teachers aren't out to scam you so don't throw out your history books just yet. As usual, the truth isn't black and white. Many of the figures in this book *were* real people. They lived and breathed, just like you and me. Only, they weren't exactly the brilliant figures we learn about in school. Some were fake; some were phony; and some were just plain made up. The people who were once real have been crushed by their own legends long ago. Today, we actually think the legends are the real deal.

They aren't.

This book isn't trying to get rid of anybody's beloved Bard or peace-loving cannibal, but it is trying to expand your knowledge about history. So if controversy makes your skin tingle and mysteries make your head ache, this may not be the book for you. But if you want to know who really wrote Homer's epics, or how Shakespeare could possibly be a big, fat phony, then dive in and enjoy another side of history's movers and shakers.

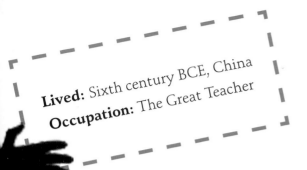

Lived: Sixth century BCE, China
Occupation: The Great Teacher

Chapter
1

Confucius

Man of Many Sayings

Popularity Contest

Today, Confucius would rule the Twitter-sphere with all his pithy sayings, just as he ruled ancient China's word game. Instead of "Do not do to others what you do not want done to yourself," Confucius's quips would read more like: *B4 U EMBARK ON A JOURNEY OF REVNGE, DIG 2 GRAVZ.* But hey, the message is still there.

Confucius lived at the same time as other great thinkers, such as Thales in Miletus and Buddha in India. Maybe it was something in the water. In any case, the sixth century BCE churned out more great thinkers than Harvard has churned out presidents.

After people in China realized the potential of the great stuff coming out of Confucius's mouth, they started flocking to him. Some say that over three thousand disciples followed him around the country. Many scholars believe it was probably closer to seventy-two (although that's even suspicious). Still, it's an impressive number before social media could help get the word out about the new guy in town.

Confucius's sayings were gathered together in a book called the *Analects*.

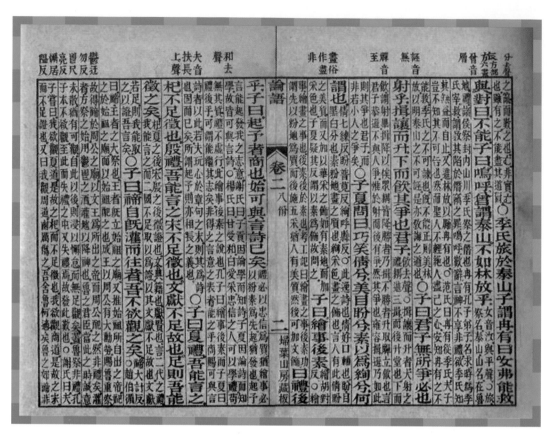

The Analects: *just don't call them an autobiography.*

The *Analects* brims with useful aphorisms—short blurbs about the best ways to live, work, and learn. At least, that's what the history books tell us. In reality, most of these sayings weren't written down until a century after Confucius lived. Not only that, but much of what we know about Confucius's life was compiled decades, and even centuries, after his death.

Who's to say this guy wasn't some old fraud?

If he was, it wasn't his fault. After Confucius died in 479 BCE, his followers started "remembering" all the great things he did: Thought up hundreds of brilliant sayings; invented a new philosophy; stood over nine feet tall; slayed a fire-breathing dragon while wearing fuzzy, pink bunny slippers. Done, done, and done.

Okay, maybe not that last one, but you can see how easily his reputation snowballed. Everyone wanted to turn this man into a legend. Maybe they just felt bad for ignoring him during his lifetime.

It isn't easy being awesome.

Confucius Who?

What's the story behind the most influential man in Chinese history? With thousands of followers, or at least a few dozen, he was probably handsome and well-spoken, right? Not really. History tells us that he was ugly and grotesquely tall, which sounds like a troll. Even his future biographers didn't try to sugarcoat the truth about his appearance—but they also had no problem bending the facts to make Confucius seem better than he probably was.

Take his birth, for instance. Legend says his birth was a divine answer to a prayer his mother made every night before bed. If she had a son, Confucius's father promised to marry her. Hence his name, **Kong,** which means "an utterance of thankfulness when prayers have been answered."

Lengthy in English, but it works in Chinese. Legend also says he was over nine feet

Kong:

Confucius is the Westernized version of Kong Fuzi, which means Master Kong, and is only one of the many ways to say his name in Chinese.

tall. Sure, he was probably a giant for his time—around six feet—but that's likely it. As for being ugly? His biographers say his head was so disfigured it could make kids cry. There's no documentation of any kids actually crying when they saw him, but they might have.

We do know that Confucius's dad had at least two wives, which would be frowned upon today but was all good back then. However, neither one of those women was Confucius's mother. Even though her prayers had been answered, Confucius's dad still hadn't married his mom, who was, in fact, a fifteen-year-old girl. It gets worse. A few years after Confucius's birth, his dad died, and his wives kicked baby Confucius and his mom to the street.

As a result, Confucius grew up poor and illegitimate. To get by, he did menial jobs like watching livestock. But he was smart—too smart for the other kids in his town. Even worse, they all knew it, too. While the other children played war games, Confucius hung out by himself or with other old souls, A.K.A. old men.

Finally, a local duke noticed him. How could he not notice a six-foot-tall kid with a weird head? After he got over Confucius's odd looks, the duke noticed something else—Confucius was sort of smart, unlike his peers. The duke put him in charge of some granaries, which was actually a pretty impressive gig since grain was used as money in sixth-century BCE China. What wasn't so impressive was having to count out tiny beads of grain all day. What Confucius really wanted—and what he spent his whole life trying to get—was a government position.

Confucius eventually settled down, married, and had some kids, all while wishing he could get into politics. He had this grand idea for China that he wanted to see come to life. Confucius lived during the Spring and Autumn Period—a precursor to the Warring States Period, whose name pretty much sums up the time—and for most of his life, the country was embroiled in chaos between the various warring lords.

Confucius wanted a peaceful, stable, and fair China. So he did the noble thing. He abandoned his wife and children and set out to teach people to honor their ancestors and to live humbly and righteously.

Confucius and his followers (Japan).

World Peace through World Domination

For the rest of his life, Confucius traveled the country looking for rulers to promote him to a government position. Unfortunately, very few of them listened to him, probably because Confucius always shot himself in the foot by saying stupid things. Instead of the benign, jolly sage that legend teaches us about, the actual Confucius didn't seem to understand people at all. When he met a new ruler, his first question was: "Can I be your master?" Most princes and dukes threw him out right then and there.

But that didn't discourage Confucius from asking more leaders to follow him. He even found a few who would listen and let him teach them, but then he messed up those opportunities, too. As soon as he got a prince's or duke's ear, he had a bad tendency to say things like, "An oppressive government is worse than a man-eating tiger." And man-eating tigers were no joke. His new students usually exiled him after that.

So Confucius roamed all over China, collecting followers but no royal students. He didn't take rejection well, either. When asked to comment on men higher up in the government food chain, he replied, "Pah! These puny creatures aren't even worth mentioning."

Luckily for Confucius, the lords refrained from removing his head, but they also didn't give his misshapen head a job. When he wasn't insulting dukes, he enjoyed hitting poor people with his cane and telling them to just die already. Maybe it made him feel better. His disciples, who were supposed to convert others to Confucius's way of thinking, weren't exempt from his anger, either. After his disciple Ran Qiu failed to convince his own ruler to act more ethically, Confucius got harsh with him. "He is my disciple no more," he supposedly said. "Beat the drum, my little ones, and attack him: you have my permission." Which almost sounds like the Wicked Witch of the West ordering her flying monkeys to attack the unsuspecting Dorothy and her friends.

governor:
Much debated. Maybe he did hold public office as the Minister of Crime, saw how ineffective it was, and developed the idea of ruling with virtue to set an example for everyone to follow.

As a result of his nasty personality, the actual Confucius had very little influence over others during his lifetime. But that just wouldn't do for his followers, so they decided to jazz things up after Confucius's death. His followers claimed that he was a **governor** and that crime virtually disappeared during his tenure. Being a governor would've been the perfect gig for Confucius to prove the truth of his ideas. Although, it probably never happened.

Sure, he was bitter. It'd be hard not to be after spending your whole life trying to teach people the best way to live while they refused to be taught. He tried to make the best of a bad situation. He insisted to others "not to be upset when one's merits are ignored: is this not the mark of a wise man?"

Confucius died at the age of seventy-two (there's that suspicious number again), and even on his death bed, he was still asking people if they would let him rule over them. He knew China would never be peaceful and stable with blockheads in charge, and in his opinion, they were all blockheads. He considered his life a total failure. It'd just be one more kick in the pants if he'd known that by the fourth century BCE, people thought he should have been king.

His followers knew it, though, and they kept traveling and writing, trying to spread the word about Confucius. That's when the embellishments to his life story started. They glossed over the nasty bits about him, which helped him rise in esteem throughout the country. There are three different versions of Confucius, and you can take your pick: the humble sage, the politically motivated sage, or the warrior sage, but each one was constructed centuries after his death.

Then just when Confucianism began to take root, the Qin dynasty took control of China. The leader ordered all books on Confucius burned. He also ordered that Confucius's followers be burned, too.

It turned out okay, though. The Qin's were soon overthrown, since, well, they were kind of brutal, and the Han dynasty took their place. The Hans happened to be big fans of Confucius and put all of his principles into the government. They even made Confucianism the main philosophy of China.

The Han set the stage for how all subsequent dynasties would rule. Turns out, Confucius had the last laugh after all.

Study Confucius, Live Long Life

So what were Confucius's principles? Mostly, he taught how to live as a *junzi* in order to create a good and peaceful China. If people (including rulers) lived virtuously, then their subjects would follow their example—so the thinking goes.

junzi:

A superior person; an individual who is morally noble and an example to others, typically a male. Sorry, ladies. Women usually got the short stick when it came to equality in the sixth century BCE.

If Confucius saw all the temples and statues to him today, he'd probably faint. Or whack people with his cane. Either way, he'd be excited.

Tian:

Heaven.

And no, the principles are not just punch lines used in bad Chinese parodies starting with "Confucius says . . .".

In order to rule, emperors had to have the Mandate of Heaven. *Tian* gave emperors their authority to rule, meaning their power and legitimacy came directly from above—unless they didn't follow Confucius's principles or behave like the early sage emperors (like Huangdi!—see chapter 11).

Then, *Tian* took the Mandate away, and the emperor could then be justifiably overthrown. It was exactly what Confucius always wanted in life: emperors following everything he said, exactly as he said it. He would've been so excited.

Some of the ideas of Confucianism were rather progressive, like how jobs should be given based on merit and not birth. Others weren't as forward thinking. For example, women didn't really matter until they became someone's wife, and then, Confucius tells them to obey their husbands and to walk on the opposite side of the street from men. Unfortunately for many Chinese women, this type of thinking defined their role in the world for hundreds of years to come.

At the heart of Confucianism are five core values—*Rén, Li, Yi, Zhi, and Xin*—and these dictated the way the Chinese ruled for centuries. They're that important. Confucianism is a very complicated system involving loyalty, kindness, and respect. But at the core of Confucianism lie *Rén* and *Li*.

Like a nineteenth-century Victorian gentleman, *Rén* is about propriety—always the right behavior in the right situation, especially when it comes to interacting with other people. *Rén* is sometimes translated as "benevolence," because it requires trying to see things from another person's point-of-view and then doing what's best for them. Picture Confucius beating poor people who never contributed to society—they needed to know their place; that's what was best for them. In all seriousness, though, *Rén* is the recognition that we need to be kind to others because we all live in a community and are connected to those around us by important relationships.

Li is about rituals—and boy was Confucius big on rituals. If you want to be a *junzi*, you have to respect social rituals in the proper way. These customs determine how one should drink tea, honor one's ancestors, and even govern a country. By practicing rituals down to the tiniest detail, you discipline your mind and your body to think and act in the right way. Pretty deep, huh?

The Five Basic Relationships of Confucianism

Confucianism is big on our relationships to others. Here are his top five relationships, with the most important person mentioned first, of course:

1. Ruler to Ruled
2. Father to Son
3. Husband to Wife
4. Elder Brother to Younger Brother
5. Friend to Friend

The trick was to know your place in this ruling system. A son always respects the father, and hopefully, the father will be deserving of that respect. But in Confucianism, the father doesn't have to be nice or kind to his son. He can even abandon his son, like Confucius did, and that son must still respect him. As you can see, it's good to be an old man in this scheme. Kind of like Confucius.

Top Five Confucius Sayings (That Would Totally Rule Twitter)

Confucius has so many great sayings it's hard to choose the best ones, but here are a few:

1. Man with one chopstick always goes hungry.
2. He who laughs last thinks slowest.
3. He who lives in glass house, dress in basement.
4. Man who farts in church sits in his own pew.

Just kidding. Those are bad "Confucius says" jokes. Here are some real Confucian sayings directly from the *Analects*:

1. To see the right and not do it is to lack courage.
2. When anger rises, think of the consequences.
3. When one rules by means of virtue it is like the North Star—it dwells in its place and all others turn towards it.
4. Do not be concerned that no one may recognize your merits. Be concerned that you may not recognize others'.
5. If you study but don't think, you'll be lost. If you think but don't study, you'll get into trouble.

Making a Legend

Yes, a man named Confucius lived and breathed fresh Chinese air in the sixth century BCE. But he certainly wasn't the sweet, wise teacher who had a pithy saying in his back pocket for every situation. That phony version of Confucius can only be attributed to his followers. After Confucius died, they raced for their pens and wrote down as many of his sayings as they could remember. They probably also invented a lot of new ones along the way. Then, they got walking. They traveled across China, spreading their form of Confucianism until it started trending.

As a result of his followers' efforts, Confucius's legacy is as important as any of the other great world teachers. You can't discuss what it means to be Chinese without discussing Confucianism. For over two thousand years, Confucianism was the official philosophy of China, meaning billions followed his teaching. Until the twentieth century, any student who wanted even a basic government position had to pass an exam on Confucian principles to make sure they knew how to govern properly.

It took a while, but a wise man once (supposedly) said, "It does not matter how slowly you go, so long as you do not stop." Fortunately for Confucius, his followers listened carefully to his words—even if they made some of them up in the first place.

Chapter 2

Lived: Eighteenth century CE, America
Occupation: Commander-in-Chief, first
President of the United States

George Washington

His High Mightiness

How to Look Like a Hero

It's time to take everything you think you know about George Washington and throw out at least half of it. You can start with his appearance. He was freakishly tall for his time at six-foot, three-inches, had a pockmarked nose from smallpox, auburn (red) hair, and was built like a quarterback. The white-haired elderly gentleman we know from the dollar bill didn't come until much later.

Washington was no dummy, though, so don't worry about that. He knew his role in the United States of America would be too great for people not to be interested in his life. He made sure to dot his i's and cross his t's. He even admitted as much when he said, "I walk on untrodden ground. There is scarcely any part of my conduct which may not hereafter be drawn into precedent."

In other words, he knew he had better at least have the shiny veneer of a hero unlike his actual veneers, which weren't shiny at all.

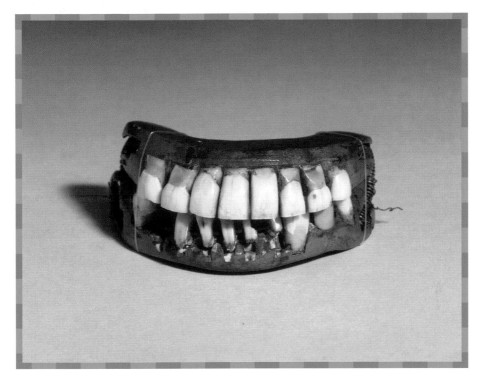

Scary enough for Halloween. Courtesy of Mount Vernon Ladies' Association

Before he was unanimously elected as general of the Continental Army (sort of), before he led the Americans to victory at Yorktown (kind of), before he graciously came out of retirement to become the first president and set the course for the new country (somewhat), George Washington was just a small-time farm boy with no professional education and a chip on his shoulder the size of Virginia.

Dr. Jekyll and Mr. Hyde

We won't even talk about the obvious fake myths surrounding George Washington, like his wooden teeth or the infamous cherry tree incident. Sure, Washington's terrible teeth could scare a zombie, but they weren't wooden. They were made from the pearly whites of humans and hippos. And he certainly could tell a lie. That sly old fox constantly covered up his secrets and misdeeds. His life depended on lying his red head off to Congress and to the British. Mostly because the entire British Empire wanted to kill him, and if they ever captured him or if the war was lost, Washington would have gotten

Bagging Bald Eagles

George considered it a good day when he was able to hunt. In true aristocratic fashion, foxes were his favorite prey, but he also got pretty excited when he shot five bald eagles and five mallard ducks in one day in 1768. For a man always worried about his historical reputation, bagging bald eagles didn't faze him. Then again, they weren't endangered yet like they are today, and the United States of America wasn't even a twinkling in his eye.

This will never go out of style!

a traitor's death—hanged, drawn and quartered.

He also wasn't the down-to-earth, calm hero everyone thinks he was. Washington tended more towards the pretentious side of Virginia aristocracy. Instead of shaking hands, he preferred to bow and would stare you down until you retracted your hand from his presence. Don't even dream of actually patting him on the back, either.

And his temper was explosive when he couldn't contain himself, although he usually could. Thomas Jefferson remembered Cabinet meeting in particular when George threw off his hat and stomped on it in a temper-tantrum most three-year-olds would envy.

George had good reasons to put on airs and fight for what he wanted. He had a lot to prove. No less than five deaths made it possible for him to become the legend we know and love. As the son of a second wife, Washington was entitled to little of his father's wealth. But with the deaths of his father, his older brother, his older brother's wife, his future wife's first husband, and his stepdaughter, Washington suddenly found himself rolling in the ***dough***.

dough:

Money. Although his face wasn't on those bills yet.

Without money, Washington wouldn't have been Washington.

It takes a lot of gold to properly clothe His High Mightiness—as he once suggested a president should be called, before deciding on the more democratic, Mr. President.

Although he came from humble beginnings, George had more refinement and class in his little pinky than the king of England had in his whole palace. At least that's what George thought. As soon as he came into some money, George made sure everyone else thought that, too.

When calling upon the Continental Congress to boycott all imported goods from Britain prior to the Revolutionary War, he secretly ordered carriages, fancy clothing, guns, and Wedgewood pottery from London for his own personal use. At another meeting of Congress, he called for the end of slavery, then went home and bought more slaves. (He preferred buying girls, so they could have kids and give him even more slaves. A sort of two-for-one deal.)

Washington was a ball of contradictions. Even in politics he wasn't always a smooth operator. He went behind people's backs, argued, and sulked. It wasn't until later in life that he learned how to hide his temper under a cool exterior. Sometimes.

Puppet Master

Washington was a master when it came to fooling people. His early career is loaded with a long list of misdeeds, including:

1. Letting his men fire the shot that started the French and Indian War.
2. (Accidentally) admitting to assassinating a French diplomat.
3. Setting up a fort in a terrible location leading to its defeat.
4. Marching against a superior force, losing, and blaming it on others.

So his first command was a dismal failure. To top it off, he quit his position because he kept getting passed over for promotion. Weird. Somehow, he still came out smelling sweeter than a rose by the time the *Second Continental Congress* needed a military leader for their army.

Second Continental Congress:

Representatives from twelve of the thirteen colonies who gathered to complain about Britain. The Declaration of Independence was signed at this gathering too, on July 4, 1776—exactly twenty-one years to the day a young George Washington lost his first fort.

(To be fair, there weren't a lot of military men to choose from. Most of the representatives from the colonies were politicians, not fighting men.)

When the French and Indian War ended, Washington was still a young guy trying to move up in a hierarchical society. After trying his hand at the military and finding "something charming in the sound of bullets" whizzing past his ears, Washington went to the dark side—politics. His first political campaign was for a seat in the *Virginia House of Burgesses.*

Virginia House of Burgesses:

As a burgess, Washington represented a county in Virginia. He had some power but was content to sit back and let the more outspoken (read: loud) burgesses like Patrick Henry ("Give me liberty or give me death!") do the talking.

Mere technicalities didn't stop George from using his imagination to gain voters. He really wanted that seat and the word "illegal" didn't faze him. Washington didn't like to lose, and after an embarrassing defeat in 1775, he stepped up his game in a big way. He had his supporters buy vats of wine, barrels of beer, and gallons of rum punch to help sway voters' opinion of him. Washington wasn't afraid to get caught buying votes. He was only afraid of not buying enough to claim victory.

He won, of course. You don't mess with colonists and their alcohol.

To make his next move up the social ladder, he had to marry, and marry well. Luckily for him, the widow Martha Dandridge Custis was better than beautiful: she was rich and she had a thing for really tall guys.

Even though his own mother boycotted his wedding, and even though George was in love with another (already married) older woman, George and Martha ended up being a match made in a miser's heaven. With their marriage, he came to own eight thousand acres at Mount Vernon and over three hundred slaves, but George didn't stop there.

He was hungrier for land than a lion for a juicy zebra rump roast, and like the previous elections, employing shady dealings didn't deter him. He secretly sent men over the invisible line dividing native and colonial lands to scout out prime real estate. When the British renegotiated a treaty allowing colonial expansion in 1768, Washington was ready to pounce.

It wasn't like he was the only one grabbing the best for himself. Most colonists were land-hungry. George was just better than most at underhanded dealings and secrecy, and he also had greater motivation for it. He knew that he would need to be pretty wealthy to get noticed by Congress. And he intended to get noticed.

Good Enough for Broadway

You might be thinking, *Sure, George wasn't the nicest guy when it came to getting what he wanted, but he had the undivided support from Congress and his fellow revolutionaries because his leadership and genius won the Revolutionary War. Men flocked to his side!*

Wrong.

The day the Second Continental Congress decided to name the head of the Continental Army, George came dressed to impress. He rolled up in his chariot and emerged in full militia uniform, despite not having been in uniform for seventeen years. Thankfully, he had a few servants at home who were handy with a sewing needle. His strategy worked. Everyone agreed—he looked the part. Washington was now the first Commander-in-Chief of the Continental Army almost by default. But A-lister looks aren't exactly a substitute for a tactical brain.

John Adams, eventually the second president of the United States, later wrote a letter stating that the "talents" that got George the general job were his "handsome face" and "tall stature." Adams forgot to mention his own part in George's success.

Stud muffin in a saddle.
Courtesy of Mount Vernon Ladies' Association

See, John Adams really didn't like John Hancock, George's chief rival for the command of the Continental Army. Maybe it was Hancock's obnoxiously large signature that Adams didn't like. Everyone knew it wasn't to make King George III take notice; it was to make Hancock popular. In order to make sure Hancock didn't become general, Adams nominated George Washington instead.

Loud and proud.

Petty differences weren't all that swayed the voters. Washington was from the South, and the delegates understood they needed to unite the colonies in order to beat the British. Washington would help to bridge the gap and tie the North and South together in one cause for freedom.

As he accepted the nomination, Washington said, "I do not think myself equal to the Command I am honored with." In this case, he wasn't being humble—he really was a terrible tactician with more "strategic retreats" than wins to date. That didn't change in the next war. But who's counting?

To solidify his reputation, he declined any payment. Instead, he magnanimously agreed to bill Congress for his expenses. Everything from liquor to spies' salaries to a broom was carefully recorded. At the end of the war, Washington charged $160,074 to the new government. That's somewhere in the millions of dollars today.

Despite being a meticulous record keeper via his thirty-two secretaries, George often found himself in debt. It might have been all those shopping sprees he enjoyed so much, but a lot of his money was also tied up in land. (He didn't get better with age when it came to money. He even had to borrow a few thousand to go to his own inauguration in New York on April 30, 1789.)

So, he wasn't good with gold, but what about his leadership qualities? Everyone must have liked him during the war once they realized what a great general he was. Right?

Wrong.

"Outgeneralled"

Washington had his army, his reputation, and his prestige. Nothing could stop him, except for the British. During 1775, Washington and the colonial army got really good at retreating. In 1776, things were going about the same way until Washington crossed the Delaware River at the end of the year and won the Battle of Trenton.

The next year, 1777, started off well for Washington and his army, with a second win at Princeton a few days into January, but then things started going downhill again with Washington racking up defeats like he was racking up a pool table. The next horrendous winter spent at Valley Forge (1777–1778), where Washington's men starved and froze to death, was merely one low point in a year of low points.

It wasn't just the British that wanted him dead. Even men in Congress were calling for his head. People had always groused about George's lack of wins, his tactical faults, and his inability to see the big picture like keeping southern cities safe. George probably wondered if it was him when his aides tried to jump ship.

One aide secretly asked another general to take over the army, and Washington faced down mutiny on three separate occasions. Alexander Hamilton, future Secretary of the Treasury, pointed out that Washington was moody, difficult to work with, and had mild abilities as a leader—but they had beef, so that might all just be bluster. Hamilton also thought Washington was indispensable to the cause, if only outwardly. The man looked really good on a white horse, and looks were important.

Truly Alarming

Despite being the poster boy for a new republic, George still had a bit of the pretentious in him. He really wanted to look elite and that meant surrounding himself with people that also looked elite. He needed an entourage. So he formed his own personal Life Guard to follow him everywhere. They made sure he wasn't kidnapped or assassinated, and they carried his personal papers.

It wasn't enough that the men in his Life Guard were muscular and good at playing postmaster. George had high standards down to every last plumed feather in their hats (because without a hat, a man's appearance was just ruined according to Washington). They had to be at least five feet, eight inches tall, wear what he told them to wear, and own property. Washington spared no expense on them, but kept the group very hush-hush. It wouldn't do for Congress to find out how expensive his kept men were. But Washington was a master of secret-keeping. He also kept an entire spy ring secret from Congress while he was general!

Despite not knowing the terrain during important battles, despite being indecisive, and despite not having that spark of genius that marks most great generals, Washington was exactly what the American cause needed: a tough-as-tacks poster boy for freedom. His superhuman ability to dodge bullets didn't hurt his image, either. Washington could come off the battlefield, his coat riddled with bullet holes, and not a scratch on him.

Somehow, even when he lost a battle, Washington still won. After the bloody Battle of Germantown (October 4, 1777), Washington lost his position and twice as many men as the British, but the French decided he was pretty brave and threw their weight behind his flailing army. (It helped that his generals were winning important battles at places like Saratoga.)

Mercifully, too, since the French were better at the whole "strategy" thing than the Americans. They had been using it against the British for a lot longer. It was thanks to French advice that the colonists won at Yorktown (1781), which was the beginning of the end for the British dream of one big Canada. It was also the beginning of Washington's celebrity status and the end of Washington's human status.

Casanova?

Washington had a habit of capitalizing on his good looks, like winning command of the army and charming French generals into helping the American cause. That's because he knew the importance of looking the part. And while his marriage was a good one, he didn't mind flirting and dancing with pretty, young girls after a few sips of champagne.

In fact, Abigail Adams, wife of John Adams, was so infatuated with him that in her letters to her husband she gushed about Washington's goodness—and his good looks. Furthermore, Lady Kitty, the daughter of one of Washington's generals, requested a lock of George's hair, and Caty Greene, wife of General Nathaniel Greene, danced for three straight hours at a ball with Washington. Afterwards, she named her son after him. That must have been some two-step!

Getting Better with Age

Okay, so George wasn't great at the whole "tactics" thing while leading the army, but he *was* really good at being strict with his troops. He was forever trying to make his soldiers look like his own personal mini-me's. He wanted them to stop gambling, drinking, and cursing. A man could get twenty-five lashes for uttering a curse word, fifty lashes for drinking, and fifteen hundred lashes for desertion. That is, until Washington had a gallows built and hanged a couple of repeat deserters as a warning to the rest of the soldiers.

Washington was constantly annoyed with his men unless they pulled off a miraculous feat, like trudging miles through snow with bleeding feet or winning against terrible odds. Then he liked them. After their shared suffering during the winter at Valley Forge—where up to ten men died a day from the cold, disease, and starvation—Washington became his soldiers' biggest supporter. He stopped complaining about how worthless his volunteers and officers were and started defending them. He may have stayed in plusher quarters and ate dinner each night, but he knew they were miserable, and he felt bad enough about it to beg, borrow, and steal things they needed.

In time, Washington grew into his position. He gave better treatment to prisoners of war, inoculated his army against smallpox, operated a spy ring, mixed *freed slaves* into his army, deleveoped a navy for the colonies, and finagled much-needed funds and arms from Congress. But it seems that the reality of the job finally hit home, and he once mentioned how he would have never taken the gig if he'd known how hard it would be.

freed slaves:

Even though Washington allowed freed slaves to fight with the army, it's not as magnanimous a gesture as it first appears. If it had been up to him, he would never have allowed them to serve. But he desperately needed men, and the British were only too happy to arm black men for their cause. So Washington reversed his decision a year into the war, and the Continental Army was the most integrated army in America until the 1960s.

Washington may have lost more battles than he won and he was usually outmaneuvered by the superior British forces, but he held the army together, inspired loyalty in his men by his bravery, and persuaded men to reenlist. That's no small accomplishment, no matter what kind of general you are.

First President—Kind Of

After the British surrendered and the Treaty of Paris was signed, Washington didn't get unanimously voted in as first president, nor did he prance into the

Oval Office as a thank-you for winning the war. For one, the first president to stay in the White House was John Adams (president number two), and the Oval Office wasn't built until 1909.

Besides that, the states had to make a few mistakes at governing before Washington took the role as president. Enter the Articles of Confederation, which gave each state a ton of power and created a bunch of presidents in what was called the Congress Assembled.

It was a terrible idea. Nobody agreed and nothing got done. So that was scrapped and the United States Constitution was born in 1787. The Constitution balanced the power between the states and the federal government. It also made one person president, and that person was none other than George Washington, who *was* unanimously voted into office.

Now—finally!—you can start picturing the white-haired, dignified-looking Washington.

You don't want to know what's behind those pursed lips . . .

Don't go crazy and start thinking he was the brains behind the operations. Washington knew enough to know he didn't know enough. So he surrounded himself with geniuses, and he didn't mind leaning on them for advice—a great tactic for once. Instead of dictating policy, like a dictator, he guided it with the wise advice of others, which became a precedent.

Even some of Washington's speeches were written by others. George never attended a university, even though he really wanted to, so spelling and grammar weren't exactly his forte. It was something that always bothered him. It also bothered one of his first historians, Jared Sparks, who went back through Washington's old letters and cleaned up the truly horrendous grammatical errors and fancified his dull sentences.

Others helped create the myth of George Washington by gussying up details about his life. The famous painting of Washington crossing the Delaware shows George heroically standing in front of the first American flag. In reality, Washington was still flying the Grand Union during the crossing—which had the British flag in the corner with stripes across its body representing the thirteen colonies—but that didn't seem as patriotic for the painter and the flag was changed to the new American flag.

Some played up Washington's Hulk-like physique, claiming that he threw a silver dollar across the Potomac River. Sadly, there were no silver dollars in circulation at the time of Washington's life, and no one could do that except for the actual Hulk.

Even the infamous cherry tree story was phony thanks to Washington's earliest biographer, Parson Weems, who apparently thought George wasn't cool enough on his own to sell books.

Washington did accomplish a lot of real things, though. He set precedents that presidents still go by today, like only serving two terms, wearing civilian clothing, giving an inaugural address, picking his inner circle, reserving evenings for dinner

Washington Today

Washington was lucky that there were no such things as televised debates and campaign speeches back in 1776. He never would've become president if there had been. He had a soft voice—John Adams sometimes had to repeat what Washington said in Congress so people could hear—and off-the-cuff questions made him nervous. Also, his dentures had the distinct possibility of falling out of his mouth whenever he spoke.

The Grand Union flag: not the patriotic look they were hoping for.

parties, and retreating back home when the job gets to be too much. (When in doubt, retreat!) He had to make tons of decisions not made explicit in the Constitution.

Washington set another precedent that seems to have been passed down through the years: leaving the next president with his really messy foreign problems.

Since the British were sore losers, they liked to take American sailors on the high seas and impress them—not by flexing their muscles or showing them the best Caribbean beaches, but by kidnapping them and forcing them into the British Navy. This was called *impressment*, and it was pretty obnoxious, but Washington didn't plan on solving the problem while in office. In fact, Washington said good luck to the second president, John Adams, and retired to Mount Vernon, leaving America open to another war with Britain—the War of 1812.

Paging Greatness

For what should George Washington be considered great? Being a good leader and politician? Being the first president of a new democracy? It's complicated since the revolution switched one set of old white guys for another set of old white guys with slightly less snobbish accents. Slaves didn't get any more rights and neither did women.

Yet, despite Washington's faults, who else in history has been asked to raise an army, stop a juggernaut (the British Empire), and start a new nation? And then after he succeeded, he did something kind of crazy. He gave up power not once, but twice.

Instead of riding into Congress and crowning himself emperor—kind of like Napoleon did a few years later in France—he handed in his title of military dictator. Then, Washington stepped down from office after two terms as president. This kind of thing sent a pretty strong message to the rest of the world.

True, he was sick of getting raked over burning hot coals by his one-time friends and prying media. He also wasn't feeling well and the last tooth in his rotten mouth was gone, but he set the *term limit* at two, which has not been changed since. There would never be a king or emperor ruling for life in the United States of America.

In the end, maybe what made Washington appear so great (and what we still remember to this day) was looking exactly how a budding new country needed its founding father to look: majestic on a horse during war, and wise and measured on a dollar bill.

term limit:

Except for Franklin D. Roosevelt who was elected four times, but only got to serve three before he died. After him, Congress quickly passed the Twenty-Second Amendment limiting term limits to two—just like George Washington.

Lived: Sixth century BCE, Greece
Occupation: Mathematician (ish)

Pythagoras

The Father of Everything

Immortality Suits Pythagoras

Are you confused by $a^2 + b^2 = c^2$? A little fuzzy on the meaning of the word *hypotenuse*? Unsure why the triangle has to be "right"? Don't worry. It's quite possible that Pythagoras was just as perplexed as you are, and he supposedly invented the formula.

Pythagoras lived around 570 BCE in Samos, an island off the coast of modern-day Turkey, and also in Croton, a city in Southern Italy. That's about all you can take to the bank. Everything else is debatable.

See, Pythagoras attracted legends like bugs to a bright light. Except, he was more like the fat spider in the corner, gobbling down legend after legend. It's hard to blame him, since he was dead for most of the meal. It was his followers who threw incredible deed after miraculous feat at the memory of the dead man, turning him into history's biggest math fraud. It wasn't just the triangle thing, either.

Pythagoras suddenly invented mathematics, discovered the secrets of the harmony of the spheres, and began Greek philosophy itself. That's a pretty impressive résumé for a corpse. But first, he taught students something a little different than your average geometry teacher.

Are you sure this is "right"?

A Vegetarian before It Was Cool

The Greeks didn't have the rosiest ideas about the afterlife. It was more doom and gloom than harps and happiness. They believed that inconsolable **shades** roamed a dark field in Hades for eternity. Shades were hungry and cold and miserable, and they stayed that way forever.

Enter Pythagoras. Like a **hoplite** in shining armor, he came to the rescue of any Greek unhappy with such a bleak picture of life after death, and really, who wouldn't be?

According to Pythagoras, you didn't have to die. Not for long, at least. You could be reborn. He swore he'd

shades:

Ghosts.

hoplite:

Greek warrior.

chiton:
Greek version of the toga.

been reincarnated four times already. He even remembered the battle at Troy where he had been killed by Menelaus centuries ago.

Like most good things in life, it wasn't easy to be reborn. It took a lot of hard work, but Pythagoras had a few tricks up his *chiton* to help his followers achieve this immortality.

If you thought life in Ancient Greece without running water and television was hard enough, becoming a Pythagorean meant life was about to get a lot harder.

Some of the easy rules included: don't eat beans, don't eat animals (that delicious goat might be your grandfather, after all), don't let yourself be buried with wool, don't stir a fire with iron, don't look in a mirror that's beside a light, don't use public roads, don't step over a yoke, and definitely don't speak in the dark. That was just the beginning, though. The list was exhaustive, and exhausting. (Hard ones involved sitting at a table full of food, letting the smell of hot, tasty roast goat waft up your nose, and then leaving without touching a thing after a "considerable time.")

Membership to Pythagoras's club was exclusive. This was a secret society of sorts. Not everyone could join, and for the first five years of membership, no one was allowed to talk, even

Don't Cross the Boss

Pythagoras liked numbers. They were pretty, they were rational, and they were magical, which just about covers all the criteria Pythagoras needed. According to legend, everything was numbers—whole numbers, to be exact. People who believed in imaginary, irrational, and negative numbers (all things mathematicians study today), well, they weren't allowed into Pythagoras's group. In fact, irrational numbers and their type were even worse than toot-inducing beans.

Unfortunately, Hippasus, one of Pythagoras's most famous followers, picked a bad time to discover the irrationality of the square root of two—on a boat in the middle of the sea. Hippasus, perhaps forgetting the bigwig didn't like irrational numbers, was understandably excited to show his findings, so he challenged his fellow Pythagoreans to find a whole number answer to the square root of two. Their bushy eyebrows scrunched together and their eyes started to cross. Nothing worked. Steam probably poured out of the Pythagoreans' ears soon after.

At this point, Hippasus should've been nervous. Word couldn't get out that there were irrational numbers, so the group (or perhaps Pythagoras himself) threw Hippasus overboard. Hippasus would have to tell his discovery to the fishes. (Just to be clear, this story was first told hundreds of years after it supposedly happened. And there are a lot of versions.)

in daylight. That's one easy way to keep people from complaining about how much they miss their mom, or not getting to take the easy way home—on a road.

So was Pythagoras the first vegetarian? Maybe, or maybe not. Some say he ate no meat and wouldn't even talk to butchers. Others say he ate meat except for oxen. Unless someone tracks down a recently reincarnated Pythagoras, his eating habits will stay a mystery. Except for the beans. His followers were very clear on that count.

No beans allowed, because not only did beans look like fetuses (and you wouldn't want to be a cannibal, would you?) but everyone knows the more beans you eat, the more you toot, and that can obviously distract you from thinking about lofty things like death and math.

The Original Renaissance Man

With such an interesting man, it didn't take long for more rumors about his life to start flying. And the golden rule of rumors is the crazier, the better. Crazy tends to grab people's attention.

How crazy, you ask? How about this: He was a son of Apollo, the god of reason; he could be in two places at once; he could predict earthquakes; he never laughed; he bit a snake to death; and he had a golden thigh—things of that nature. Things teachers really should mention in math class more often.

In his lifetime, Pythagoras only claimed to know mystical secrets about the hereafter. A few hundred years later, and people claimed Pythagoras knew everything. (Saying he was the son of a god probably helped sway disbelievers.) It was thanks to these rumors

Snake and beans: it's what's for dinner.

Harmonizing Hammers: the opposite of MythBusters.

and to his loyal followers, that Pythagoras was soon the Father of Everything.

By the fourth century BCE, things had spiraled out of control. Somebody insisted Pythagoras discovered musical harmony simply by walking past a blacksmith's forge. The ringing of the hammers sounded pleasant—except for one. Pythagoras ran inside, only to realize the one unharmonious hammer didn't have any ratios in common with the others. Thus, the principle of harmony was found, even though the MythBusters could debunk this in a second.

Next, Pythagoras was declared the Master of Philosophy, right about the time some famous guy named Plato was writing down his own philosophical conversations (427–347 BCE). Pythagoras's followers cried foul and accused Plato of plagiarism.

As for the famous Pythagorean Theorem, it wasn't until the first century BCE that the two become connected by a Roman. Cicero said that Pythagoras found something new and sacrificed an ox. Then Cicero had to go and say he didn't believe the stories. Every writer after Cicero conveniently left out the "I do not believe it" bit and embellished the story, including Vitruvius thirty years later, who added the all-important triangle bit.

According to an earlier source—now lost—a guy named Apollodorus the Calculator (Not to be confused with Apollodorus the Tape Measure. Just kidding.) mentioned how Pythagoras celebrated the secret of triangles not by going out for ice cream, but by sacrificing oxen—which later got turned into a *hecatomb*. Which seems like it would get in the way of that vegetarian thing. Maybe that's why Cicero said he didn't believe it.

Nothing stopped Pythagoras's reputation from snowballing. People began to attribute all sorts of math-y things to him. They would write out their own findings and sign Pythagoras's name at the bottom in a sort of reverse form of plagiarism. They hoped attaching his name would give their ideas more legitimacy. Today, it'd be like writing a groundbreaking essay on the power of baking soda for science fair volcanoes and then signing both your name and *Marie Curie's* name as the authors.

Your teacher has to give you an A, right? *Marie Curie* helped you write the essay.

Just to be clear, Pythagoras had about as much to do with all of these discoveries as a bean.

hecatomb:
A hundred cows, give or a take a few moos.

Marie Curie:
A famous nineteenth- and twentieth-century chemist who got a little too friendly with deadly chemicals.

Just like Nessie

The real Pythagoras is as elusive as the Loch Ness monster, and just like Nessie, he's been giving us the slip for thousands of years. That's because the most detailed stories of Pythagoras come from men living in the third century CE. When you do the math, that's eight hundred years after Pythagoras kicked the bucket (for the fifth time, at least, according to him).

It was like a massive game of telephone. If a story can change in only a few minutes, imagine how much it can change in a few hundred years. The later writers looked at earlier sources and came to their own conclusions, which is what you call really bad research.

Diogenes Laertius used earlier sources such as Plato and Aristotle. He wrote about 200 CE and mentioned a guy named Pythagoras who had a bunch of followers, who found the answer to a right triangle, and who sacrificed a hecatomb upon its discovery.

Iamblichus, a Syrian philosopher from 300 CE, had a bit of a different agenda. If Pythagoras had been alive to hear his words, his head would've swelled so much it might have exploded. Iamblichus claimed that Pythagoras invented political education, coined the word "philosophy," and overthrew despots (in addition to all the math stuff, of course). According to Iamblichus, Pythagoras knew how to talk with bulls, and he was really handsome. Obviously. You don't get to be that famous without being good looking.

However, it wasn't just people in the ancient world fighting to be president of the Pythagoras fan club. In 1632, Galileo got in on the action. In his famous treatise, *Dialogue on the Two Chief World Systems,* he claimed that Pythagoras first discovered the proof for a right triangle.

This is a how a legend is born, but just because it's old and passed on for hundreds of years, doesn't mean it's true. In fact, it probably means the opposite. It seems that the only thing Pythagoras did really well was to trust his followers to spread the good news about him.

The Real Reason Hippasus Got the Boot

The Pythagoreans were split into two sides: the *acusmatici* and the *mathêmatici.* The *acusmatici* emphasized the religious ideas Pythagoras was known for and all those crazy rules. The *mathêmatici* preferred math and numbers. Both claimed to be the closest to Pythagoras's true teachings, and as a result, things got nasty between the two groups. The *acusmatici* accused the *mathêmatici* of really descending from Hippasus and his love of numbers. The *mathêmatici* denied it and figuratively threw Hippasus under the bus. (And this was after they threw him over the side of the boat! Poor Hippasus.) No one liked Hippasus anymore even though he is the first mathematician and music theorist in the Pythagorean tradition, at least that we know of. That's what you call the raw end of a deal.

The Common Denominator

So we do know one more thing for certain: Pythagoras was the head of a religious cult, and not the leader of a bunch of nerdy guys sitting around scratching math equations in the dirt with a stick. Attributing all those discoveries to him would be like claiming Buddha discovered the theory of relativity. Sorry, Einstein.

So why study a man who clearly had nothing to do with inventing the Pythagorean Theorem and who probably didn't even give a hoot about math?

Because Pythagoras was a superstar during his time and for centuries after. Instead of being known for singing catchy tunes or throwing wild parties, he was known as a shaman. He influenced scores of people—the Pythagoreans—and Western thought for generations to come, even if he didn't do a lot of that thinking himself. When math students learn about the history behind their equations, his name is *still* one of the most common in textbooks.

When Copernicus was studying the earth's relationship to the sun, he didn't name his findings after himself, but after Pythagoras. (Sound familiar?) He originally called his findings, *Astronomia Pythagorica*. (It wasn't until later that the world started calling them the *Copernican Revolution*.) Copernicus's findings started the sixteenth century Scientific Revolution, two thousand years after Pythagoras lived; but somehow, Pythagoras still gets at least partial credit.

Liar, liar, chiton on fire.

Obviously, someone had to discover the theorem of the right triangle, even if it wasn't Pythagoras. So who was it? Well, scholars don't exactly know. Some cuneiform tablets seem to prove that the Babylonians knew about the whole triangle business at least a thousand years before Pythagoras was even born. The Chinese and Indians were all over geometry, too. There wasn't a ton of contact between these cultures at the time, so it's doubtful that they copied each other. They probably each discovered it independently.

The first known proofs of the theorem come from *The Elements* by Euclid, another famous Greek living about 250 BCE (or did he? We have no evidence on him either). Clearly, the Greeks loved their numbers.

Leguminophobia?

Pythagoras probably had an eventful life, even if scholars don't actually know what the events were. Perhaps the most enduring legend around Pythogoras's life centers on the way he died—by beans. That's like someone with anthophobia (a fear of flowers) accidentally brushing up against a petunia and dying from an allergic reaction. Guess they were right to be afraid.

According to the story, Pythagoras's cool kids' club had started to rub people the wrong way. It was secretive, exclusive, and a bit spooky with all its mysticism. So one night, some disgruntled locals decided to do something about the weird hippie living down the street. Setting his house on fire seemed like a good solution.

Pythagoras managed to escape, only as someone with his head in the clouds all day he didn't know his neighborhood very well. He took off with the pyromaniacs in hot pursuit and ran straight into a bean field. When he realized his mistake, he refused to take one step farther, even if it meant escape. Instead, Pythagoras screamed that he would rather die by savages than trample beans, and so he did.

Hopefully, when he was reborn, it wasn't as a bean farmer's son.

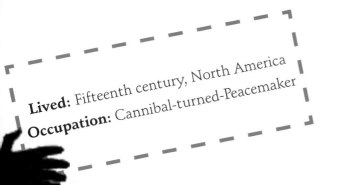

Lived: Fifteenth century, North America
Occupation: Cannibal-turned-Peacemaker

Chapter

4

Hiawatha

Incarnation of Wisdom

Scrambled Names

If you're into nineteenth-century poetry (and who isn't?), then you may at first confuse our Hiawatha, creator of the Iroquois Confederacy, with the Hiawatha of Henry Wadsworth Longfellow's poem, *The Song of Hiawatha*. Easy mistake. It turns out that even Longfellow, the famous American poet, was confused. His poem details—in typical Romantic exaggeration—the exploits of men from the Chippewa tribe, possibly one in particular named Manabozho, but he called him Hiawatha of the Iroquois. Which is a little like confusing a New Zealander for an Aussie. Big mistake.

Longfellow thought the name Hiawatha was another nickname for the Chippewa man. He also thought it sounded cooler and more poetic than Manabozho, which is debatable. Longfellow's Hiawatha had lots of adventures, like slaying evil magicians and inventing writing, but eventually he saw the light and became Christian. *Our* Hiawatha did no such things.

So while Longfellow's Hiawatha never existed, the real Hiawatha (possibly) did and so (possibly) did his buddy, the Great Peacemaker. Together, this dynamic duo brought peace to the various Iroquoian tribes and created the first republic—something the American Founding Fathers copied for their own republic as brazenly as a schoolyard bully before class.

cannibals:

They enjoy tasty morsels of their fellow human beings.

Through centuries of retelling his story, the real Hiawatha got lost under the weight of Longfellow's poem and his own legends. Legends filled with *cannibals* and murderers. As usual, the truth has a hard time competing with cannibals. The world hasn't known the real Hiawatha since.

Reforming a Cannibal

Before we get to the cannibals, however, you're probably wondering how the Great Peacemaker got such an awesome nickname when his real name was Dekanawida. Well, it certainly wasn't by killing and eating people. Even as a kid, Dekanawida refused to play any violent, war-like games. Instead, he preferred talking about his feelings and hanging out with his mom to throwing sticks at kids' heads.

Yes, the Great Peacemaker was always destined for greatness. The prophecy at his birth even said so. The prophecy also claimed that he would bring about the end of his people, the Hurons, for his efforts. His grandmother didn't like the sound of that and took a couple cracks at killing Dekanawida when he was an infant. Don't worry, none of the attempts stuck, but his people still didn't trust him. It didn't help that he stammered when he got excited.

When Dekanawida grew up, he left the Huron people to preach peace to other tribes. His stuttering, however, squashed that dream. Through the grapevine, Dekanawida heard of a great medicine man who had lost his entire family to a murderer. In his grief, the medicine man had become a hermit. Oh yeah, he also ate people.

Before the cannibal thing got in the way, this man preached peace, just like Dekanawida. Better yet, he didn't stammer. Dekanawida saw a great opportunity in this hermit; the bad habit of boiling limbs was just a minor roadblock. The hermit, of course, was named Hiawatha.

The Great Peacemaker sought him out, hoping to change Hiawatha's mind and become his partner in peace, despite the fact that Hiawatha was busy stewing human limbs in his crockpot. It was definitely a strange first meeting for a couple of guys interested in peace. Luckily, it didn't take much convincing for Hiawatha to put down the femur and follow Dekanawida into the light.

So to whom exactly were Hiawatha and Dekanawida planning on preaching? (Hint: it's not the choir. Mostly because Christianity and their choirs didn't arrive in North America until much later.)

Women in Charge

Thanks to culturally insensitive Euro-pean explorers and their "dear diaries," history thinks of North America as a *Disney movie*.

We imagine a pure land where the inhabitants skipped around picking ber-ries all day, hung out with animals, and lived in bliss before the white settlers arrived.

Disney movie:

The one where Pocahontas and all her animal friends canoed down lazy rivers and ran around meadows singing happy songs. P. S. Talking willow trees and pet raccoons were never normal in North America.

This is false. The native tribes of North Amer-ica had human problems, just like the incoming white settlers, because, they were human, just like the white settlers. (Although some Europeans convinced themselves those super tanned natives might not actu-ally be human.)

With regular problems like murder and revenge in the pure land of North America, it was up to two guys to form a *multi-nation alliance* between the tribes.

multi-nation alliance:

It's hard to put an exact date on this pact, but it usually ranges from 1100 to 1660. Yes, this is a big range, which means no one knows.

In this pre-settler time, the people living in what is now upstate New York weren't much different than the Italians with their vendettas in the same period. Five tribes in particular were in a constant state of murder and revenge. We call them the Iroquois today, even though Iroquois is really a shared language and custom. The people who spoke it called themselves *Haudenosaunee*, which means Peo-ple of the Longhouse. As you can probably guess, they lived in long houses.

Grandma's in charge.

Their lives centered on these longhouses, where multiple generations of one family lived in a single wooden structure. Sometimes up to sixty people lived together. Grandma lived in the front of the house, and she was always in charge because this was a matrilineal society. Matrilineal, in a nutshell, means that women tell the men where to be, when to be there, and what to do once they get there. When a man got married, he moved in with his wife's family—at the back end of their longhouse.

The system worked out great. Men went off to war and hunted, while women got down to the business of running the village. But the relentless warfare against their fellow Iroquois was seriously getting in the way of living.

The Great Law of Peace

All Hiawatha and Dekanawida had to do was get five separate tribes to agree to meet at a council. The five tribes included the Mohawk, the Oneida, the Onondaga, the Cayuga, and the Seneca. History doesn't know for sure, but Hiawatha was either a Mohawk or an Onondaga.

The two men traveled to each tribe to speak with their sachems (chiefs) and explain their plan for peace.

Each tribe could stay separate—that was most important. This Great Peace would connect the tribes through their shared culture and language, but each tribe would remain distinct. The whole point was to stop burying the *hatchet* in each other and bury it under the White Tree of Peace instead.

hatchets:
Before white settlers, hatchet weren't really used in war. They killed each other with spears, clubs, and arrows.

If a problem arose that affected all the tribes, a Great Council would be called. Each tribe would send their elected sachems to voice their tribe's concerns. The sachems were men, but the women did the electing (and de-electing, if necessary) and before the sachems left, the women told them what to say at the meeting. The council would then collectively decide how to solve the conflict. They also would decide other things, like who they should make war on when the five tribes agreed on peace. (The Algonquins and Hurons were always a popular choice.)

The League of the Iroquois was sort of like the United Nations of today: separate nations coming together to solve shared problems—except with no nuclear weapons.

All the tribes seemed to be on board with this new league except for the sticky issue of revenge killings. If the tribes all lived in peace, what happened when someone was murdered? Fortunately, Hiawatha had an answer for this dilemma.

It's hard to put a price on a human life, but Hiawatha managed fine enough. He figured that ten strings of *wampum* beads per male and twenty per female ought to cover the cost of any murdered person. An extra twenty beads would even save the killer's own life.

laws:
Today, a reading of the Great Laws can take up to four eight-hour days. That's a lot of laws.

Beads may not sound like a lot to you, but they were the hot commodity of the day. The beads weren't used as money, but instead, *wampum* beads were traded and were used to propose marriage. They could even be woven together like a belt to tell a story, to show authority, to signify an adoption, to carry a message, or to stand as a memory aide when remembering all of Hiawatha and Dekanawida's *laws*.

They were the perfect thing to give in retribution for a murder, and it was way better than an endless cycle of revenge killings.

The laws set down by Hiawatha and Dekanawida provided the foundation for the League of the Iroquois (also called the Iroquois Confederacy). The Wampum Belt showed the five nations with a line connecting them, but never running through them. Equal, but separate. The stage was set; peace was so close the two men could practically taste it.

The last thing standing in their way was a man Hiawatha knew a little too well—a nasty sort of fellow named Tadodaho, and a fellow cannibal. The cannibal thing wasn't the reason why Hiawatha knew him. There was no "I heart brains and hearts club." No, they knew each other because Tadodaho had murdered Hiawatha's family.

He struck more fear into the Iroquois than finding a worm lurking in that apple you're about to nosh on. None of the other tribes wanted to join in the Great Law of Peace because Tadodaho promised to make their life miserable if he let them live at all. And the tribes couldn't just give Tadodaho the cold shoulder—he might decide to eat that shoulder instead.

Dekanawida suggested that Hiawatha convince Tadodaho to join the league by talking to him. Probably because it takes one to know one, and by

A modern-day Hiawatha belt made of wampum beads illustrating the League.

that, Dekanawida meant they were both as disturbed as Hannibal Lector (yet another cannibal).

It Takes One to Know One

Practically Medusa.

Hiawatha was understandably nervous as he and Dekanawida approached Tadodaho to discuss the league with him. According to legend, the guy had snakes living in his hair and he was munching on a victim right then and there. If the talk didn't go well, he might decide to make them a part of the menu with a side of olive branch. Dekanawida knew he'd be fine—he was too handsome to be killed. Hiawatha, on the other hand, had reasons to be afraid, since this *was* the man who killed his whole family.

Hiawatha proceeded very carefully as he approached Tadodaho. He began by using his lyrical voice to sooth the monstrous man, which got him close enough to discover the problem. Turns out, Tadodaho had relentless headaches caused by all that pent-up meanness. Since Hiawatha used to be a medicine man, he made some tea for him to drink and combed the snakes out of Tadodaho's hair. Tadodaho, in turn, realized that he was tired of war and revenge, and of not having any friends. It didn't take long for Hiawatha to talk him into joining their league as none other than the official host of the council—called the fire keeper.

Tadodaho accepted, and soon all five tribes met at the first Council of the Great Peace. Legend has it, right after their work was complete, Dekanawida paddled out into a lake and was never seen again. Where he paddled to in a lake is anyone's guess. Hiawatha hung around to help keep that peace alive.

It all makes for a great story, except that none of that stuff probably happened that way. Especially the cannibal parts. Sorry.

A Giant Game of Telephone

Horatio Hale:
An American scientist who studied native populations.

History will never know if a reformed cannibal named Hiawatha and his miraculously handsome partner, Dekanawida, ever existed in real life since their story wasn't recorded until the late nineteenth century by *Horatio Hale*.

It's safe to say that their names were sung around campfires in the *Haudenosaunee* oral tradition for centuries. Through the centuries the legends got wilder. This is probably how the cannibalism accusations got started—not because it was true, but because it sounded like it could be true, and it made the story better.

ethnologists:
People who study differences in cultures.

In fact, some *ethnologists* believe Hiawatha and Dekanawida represent multiple people, and they don't mean guys with split personalities.

Instead, quite a few historical men helped the whole peace and unity thing along and through years of storytelling, they morphed into those two. It's always easier to remember less, rather than more.

However many people it took, they made life good for the *Haudenosaunee*. The councils met, the sachems worked the tribes' problems out, and all the laws were kept in memory by the wampum belts. The laws of Hiawatha and Dekanawida were passed down from generation to generation. The Iroquois could still make war on their neighbors, like the Hurons, but they had peace in their immediate territories.

Then came the Europeans—the French, Dutch, and English to be exact—and they brought all their friends to the party (not just actual friends, but smallpox, measles, guns, and rum too). The results weren't good for the native populations.

You could say the Native Americans were decimated, but that would be an understatement. Decimated means one in ten are killed, which is a lot, but it's nothing compared to being octodec-imated, or even novemdecimated. It's estimated that eight in ten, or even nine in ten, native peoples were killed in the first fifty years of continuous contact with European colonists.

Luckily for the Iroquois tribes, their influential league helped them survive the losses, mostly due to their ship-tight inner workings, just the way Hiawatha wanted it.

The council was divided into three parts. The center nation, the Onondagas, kept the council fire and hosted all the other nations. The "Older Brothers" (Mohawks and Senecas) discussed the issue until they came to an agreement. Then, the "Younger Brothers" (Oneidas and Cayugas) would do the same. If everyone agreed, the matter was

Fulfilling a Prophecy

The Hurons—Dekanawida's people—never joined the Iroquois Confederacy. That was all well and fine until the Dutch arrived. In order to get as many beaver pelts and other furs as possible, the Dutch traded things like guns and whiskey to the Iroquois. This created a power imbalance among the tribes, as now the Iroquois could really do some damage to their enemies, who only had bows and arrows as defense.

The Mohawks and Senecas attacked the Hurons while the Hurons were recovering from a smallpox epidemic—in the middle of winter, no less. The Mohawks and Senecas were mad that the Hurons had been secretly making treaties with the Cayugas and Onondagas behind their back. The sick Hurons didn't stand a chance. A few villages put up resistance, but it didn't take long for the Huron nation to run for their lives. Most died, some escaped to other tribes, and others were actually adopted by the Iroquois.

And so, ironically, Dekanawida's great peace plan, the Iroquois League, ultimately destroyed his own people, just as his grandmother knew would happen.

sanctioned by the fire keepers, the Onondagas. If not, then the Onondaga fire keeper, named Tadodaho in honor of the original, would hear both sides and cast the tie-breaking vote. If a consensus still couldn't be reached, then each nation agreed to handle the issue in a way that wouldn't compromise the league.

Despite the natives' plummeting populations during this time, the Iroquois Confederacy remained powerful. They mowed down their enemies and adopted survivors as their own. Soon, they were in control of upstate New York and parts of what is now Canada, about forty thousand square miles. It sounds like a good thing, but it turned out to be not so great. Mostly because it isn't hard to spot a giant. Same goes for the Iroquois. Once the Europeans had the tribes in their sights, it didn't matter how geographically strategic their locations were, or how well their councils worked. They were doomed.

Opposites Don't Always Attract

The white settlers and native populations were about as different as video games and hide-n-go-seek. Communal farming was the way of life for the Iroquois. To the settlers, land was for individuals, and the more land one had, the better. Their dictionaries had different definitions of pretty much everything.

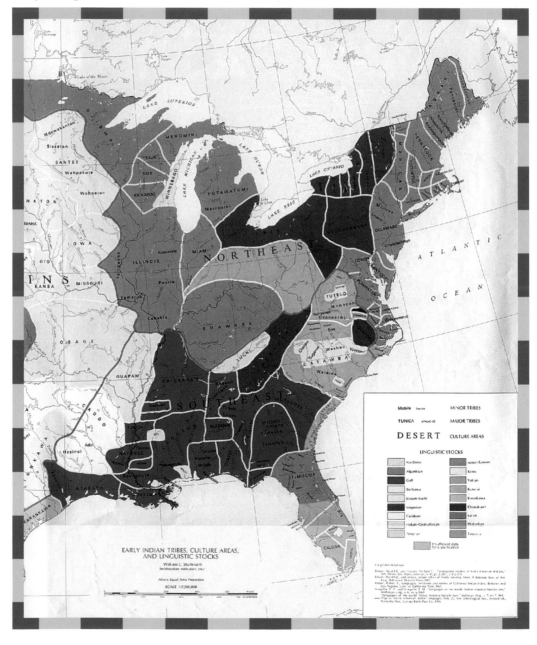

Purple marks the spot.

When the French and Indian War rolled around (1753–1763), the Iroquois backed the English. Contrary to its name, the French and Indian War wasn't actually between the French and the Native American Indians. Rather, it was a war between the French and the British with different tribes supporting either France or Britain.

For centuries, these two European powers hadn't seen eye to eye. More like knife to eye. North America was just the latest place to take their battle. The British won, thanks largely to the Iroquois, and the French retreated. Instead of New France, New England survived.

During these wars, the Iroquois absorbed other tribes and refugees devastated by all the diseases and fighting, like the Tuscaroras. Now there were six tribes in the Iroquois Confederacy and all of them formed one really bad habit. No, not picking their noses in public and dining on boogers. The tribes had absorbed colonist culture over the years, making the entire Iroquois nation dependent on the settlers for things like flint, wool blankets, and guns. Even the wampum beads were worthless after white settlers started using machines to make porcelain beads. This is where it gets bad.

After years of trading, the white settlers wouldn't accept wampum as a form of payment and that left the natives with nothing to trade except their land, which dwindled away. The giant was slowly dying.

Then came the death blow. You can call it the American Revolution. The Iroquois League was divided, unlike the colonists who were finally united in something—their hatred of Britain. Some tribes wanted to continue supporting the English, who treated them marginally better than the American farmers. Most wanted neutrality, but British and American agents made that impossible. And despite their tight-fitting breeches and bug-infested powdered wigs, those white men were really good at killing.

The League split like a log, which was exactly the opposite of what Hiawatha would have wanted. The Oneidas and some Tuscaroras sided with the colonists, but the rest backed the British, and we all know how that turned out. Backing a loser is never a good thing. When the British got booted from the colonies, it was only a matter of time before the People of the Longhouse followed.

One illegal treaty after another deprived the Iroquois of their ancestral lands. The colonists' terrible idea of a thank-you included taking land from the tribes who sided with them and slaughtering the tribes who didn't. Nothing gets a message across like a few balls of fire rolling toward a wooden home.

Most Iroquois got the not-very-subtle message and retreated to Canada and northern New York, where the Iroquoian reservations to this day function under the laws of Hiawatha and Dekanawida's legend. After centuries of power and peace, the Iroquois had lost everything—except their belief in the laws set down by their heroes.

White Men in White Wigs Always Get the Credit

How much did the league and its Great Law actually influence the fledging United States government? The two entities are obviously similar, but it's still an ongoing debate. Benjamin Franklin did say, "It would be a very strange thing if Six Nations of Ignorant Savages should be capable of . . . forming such a union . . . and yet such a union should be impractical for ten or a dozen English colonies." That's what you call a double whammy. Not only were the Iroquois considered "ignorant savages," but the colonists were even more ignorant for not being able to do what the Iroquois did.

Eventually, Thomas Jefferson took up the banner. He plucked ideas from the English Bill of Rights, Common Law, and ancient Greece and Rome. He wove them together to create something new. But the colonists also took cues from the Iroquois, such as representative government, checks and balances of power, the importance of a constitution, and interpreters of the law for their own government. So while many ideas and people influenced the United States Constitution, it's important not to overlook the importance of Hiawatha's vision.

Jefferson wasn't the only white man cherry picking all of the good stuff about the Iroquois Confederacy for his ideal government. All the way across the pond, two German philosophers, Karl Marx and Friedrich Engels, were also intrigued by reports of the Iroquoian way of life.

Their reaction was sort of the opposite of what most white men thought. Community living and sharing? Sign them up! So they each wrote a book on how everyone should live closer to the Iroquoian ideal of life.

A few years later, Soviet leaders decided to model their new government from these books (and, as such, from the Iroquois). That means that two future rivals—the United States of America and the Soviet Union —both drew inspiration for their government and their societies from the Iroquois Confederacy.

Thanks, Hiawatha. Even if you weren't a cannibal, and even if you weren't real, the stories about you were real enough to change the world.

Roman, European . . . It's Uncannily Similar

Europeans in the eighteenth and nineteenth centuries liked to categorize civilizations according to how similar they looked to their own people. On the totally made up scale of "civilized or not," they ranked people either "savage, barbaric, or civilized." If you had servants to prop up your feet whenever you rang a bell, congratulations! You were civilized. If you lived in a communal housing situation and shared everything like the Iroquois, well you were still in the "savage" stage of development.

At the time, people used these theories to explain why some people (Europeans like themselves) were better off than other people (Indians and Africans like the ones they conquered). They must not have noticed all the poverty and misery in their own societies from their darkened carriage windows.

As bad as that sounds, they weren't the first to rank people. When the Greco-Roman travel writer/geographer/historian, Strabo, explored the world in the first century BCE to the first century CE, he based a people's moral worth on how much Roman civilization they had. Less Roman influence equaled less worth. Some things never change.

Lived: Twenty-seventh century BCE, Mesopotamia
Occupation: King of Uruk, Demigod, Political Pawn

Chapter
5

Gilgamesh
Two-Thirds Divine

If It Looks Like a Legend, Smells Like a Legend, and Walks Like a Legend . . .

Gilgamesh the king is remembered best for slaying monsters and being a royal pain in the butt. He annoyed everyone from his subjects to the Mesopotamian gods before they decided to put his hero capacity to the test. When he passed with flying colors, he conveniently became every wannabe-king's long-lost ancestor.

Yes, in his day, Gilgamesh was a megastar. But that day was a long time ago and humans sort of forgot about him—until 1872.

The setting was Victorian London. The dark, musty-smelling archives of the British Museum housed thousands of baked clay tablets with weird lines that looked a lot like chicken scratches. But they weren't. They were cuneiform, a type of ancient writing that people had stopped using 1,700 years ago. These tablets had sat untranslated for years at the museum, and it wasn't until one persistent research assistant, George Smith, got down to the eye-ruining work of deciphering those chicken scratches that the ancient king re-awoke.

One day, George was reading at a table stacked high with tablets when one fragment of baked clay sang to him.

Words like "flood" and "boat" and "animals" jolted him up like a bucket of ice water down the neck. Thinking he had found confirmation of the Biblical story of Noah's ark, George forgot all about his stuffy Victorian ways. He started jumping up and down and undressing himself as if ice cubes really had gone down his neck.

Queen Victoria would not have approved.

The tablet George had found was a fragment from the *Epic of Gilgamesh* and the

A loud-mouthed soprano is in there somewhere, just waiting to be discovered.

finding would eventually shake Victorian society's beliefs in their precious Greek poet Homer—the original king of epic stories.

So who was this Gilgamesh, hero of Sumer? How did the real man ever get mixed up with the demons and monsters of the epic? And was this really a reference to the same flood of the Bible?

Spielberg Worthy

Gilgamesh was the son of a king and a goddess, which certainly helped his hero status. According to the legend, Gilgamesh had more of his mom than his dad in him, and we're not talking about eye shape. He was two-thirds divine and only one-third human. Gilgamesh couldn't get over how cool he was, and he didn't let anyone else get over it either.

A reconstructed Ziggurat of Ur. Demigods not included.

He went around town—the ancient city of Uruk to be precise—doing whatever he wanted. That included stealing other men's girlfriends and making his people participate all day in meaningless competitions. It would be fair to say that he was history's first badly behaved royal.

Eventually, his subjects couldn't take it anymore. They started grumbling—loudly. Gilgamesh wasn't so cool or funny to them anymore, and they wanted their girlfriends back. They prayed to their gods at the city's ziggurat, and for once, their prayers were answered. The gods agreed: Gilgamesh was too big for his britches (or in the case of ancient Uruk, his sheepskin loincloth).

The gods put their heads together and came up with a plan to teach Gilgamesh some humility. They created a wild man, more beast than human, who was equal to Gilgamesh in strength. They named the man Enkidu and turned him loose on the countryside.

Mayhem broke out in the forests around Uruk, and hunters began to complain to Gilgamesh, begging him to do something about Enkidu. The gods rubbed their hands in anticipation. Finally, the king would get just what he deserved—someone else equal to him in the annoying department. But Gilgamesh didn't have to think long. He knew that only one thing could stop this hairy beast-man—a woman. He chose Shamhat. She only needed a week before she had Enkidu wearing clothes, walking on two legs (instead of four), and even singing.

After he had been tamed, Enkidu walked right into Uruk, sought out Gilgamesh, and professed his undying loyalty. Some versions say the two wrestled first, but either way, they soon became fast friends. Together, they did all sorts of things best friends in Mesopotamia did, like slaying forest monsters, irritating a goddess, and fending off more beasts sent by the irritated goddess.

The gods decided that Gilgamesh must pay for his flippant attitude, and the only way to get even with him was to kill his best friend. When Enkidu died, Gilgamesh decided to undertake a quest for immortality. That dying business wasn't his thing.

His quest took him all over the known world and even into the Underworld. According to rumor, the man who had survived the Flood, Utnapishtim, was granted immortality, and Gilgamesh was determined to find him and make him spill his secrets.

After a long search, Gilgamesh found Utnapishtim and his wife and, in his usual brash manner, demanded the secrets of the gods. So Utnapishtim played along. He told Gilgamesh that if he could stay awake for six days and seven nights, then he might be able to overcome death. Gilgamesh agreed, then promptly fell asleep for a full week. Of course he tried to deny it, but the writing was on the wall. Or rather, on the moldy bread left out each day by Utnapishtim's wife to mark the time.

By the end of the epic, Gilgamesh finally realized he could never outwit death and accepted life as it came.

Historicity: Just a Fancy Word for What Really Happened

What would ever make people think that a story like this could be true? As it turns out, it was more chicken scratches. In 1922, a real outdoorsy guy named Herbert Weld-Blundell dug up a four-sided tablet called a prism in the sands of an ancient city-state. It made everybody's eyes pop out of their head when it went on display.

This is the Flood *tablet, but you already knew that if you're fluent in chicken scratches.*

Maggots tell no lies.

The Weld-Blundell Prism (catchy name, huh?) listed the names of every king in Sumer from the shadowy beginnings of life to 1800 BCE, which was when the tablet was written. Guess who made the list? That's right, Gilgamesh the King of Uruk. But if you think this settled the matter of his existence, you're wrong.

The lengths of the kings' reigns were longer than the most boring class you've ever had to sit through. According to the list, kings ruled for as long as 43,000 years and although some classes may *feel* that long, it's an impossible amount of time for humans to imagine living. Compared to these early kings, Gilgamesh's reign was pretty reasonable, clocking in at a measly 126 years.

Maybe imagining Gilgamesh as a real king wasn't so crazy. Later excavations turned up pottery shards with his name as well as other names from the king list. Archaeologists even found walls around Uruk dating to the time when Gilgamesh supposedly had them built.

At the very least, these findings suggest that a king named Gilgamesh may have existed, become extremely famous, built walls to defend his town, and as these things tend to happen, accumulated legends and admirers like barnacles on a ship. He was deified by 2500 BCE, and since then, the world has never known what's fake, and what isn't.

The truth is, there are no contemporary sources from Gilgamesh's time to prove his existence. Unless more evidence turns up, the reality of Gilgamesh could go either way. But scholars will probably argue about it for years to come, if you're interested in that sort of thing.

All those tablets do confirm something: Mesopotamia had a lot of kings.

It's Not Done Yet!

Remember all those stacks of tablets in the British Museum that were found in the 1870s? Well, they're still there, and many are waiting patiently to be deciphered. In early 2014, the assistant keeper of cuneiform tablets at the British Museum, Irving Finkel, announced he found the blueprint to the Babylonian ark. Turns out, Utnapishtim's ark would have been round and a bit smaller than a soccer field. The "blueprint" is really just another clay tablet describing the dimensions of the boat that Gilgamesh's poets decided to leave out, probably so they didn't bog down the excitement of Gilgamesh's week of sleep. Some think this is where the writers of Noah's ark got their idea—from Utanpishtim's ark.

Who knows, you could be the next person to discover a huge breakthrough in the legend of Gilgamesh. It could be you who jumps up and down and takes your shirt off in celebration—just like George Smith.

Getting into the Legend Business Isn't Easy, but Someone's Got to Do It

So if Gilgamesh was a real king and not some legendary phony, how did he turn into a superhuman character in an epic story?

Enter a king with a head for business.

Shulgi was the second king in the **third dynasty of Ur**, which means he ruled the city from 2094–2047 BCE.

He had a big man crush on Gilgamesh, whose name was still floating around six hundred years after his supposed reign. Since we have no existing fragments from this period, we don't know

third dynasty of Ur:

Lots of big stuff happened in the third dynasty of Ur (monsters and demi-gods not included). Most of it happened thanks to Shulgi, who created a standing army, a calendar, and standardized boring administrative records—dull but necessary, if you're going to be a successful ruler.

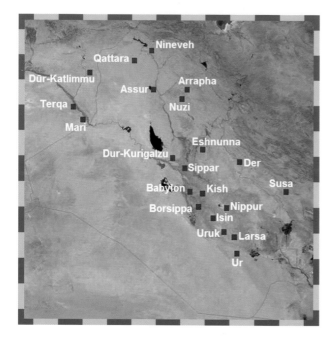

Ancient Mesopotamia circa Shulgi the Avenger's reign.

exactly what people were saying about Gilgamesh, but clearly they were talking. All Shulgi wanted was for people to think about Shulgi when they told Gilgamesh stories.

What better way to have his lowly subjects make the connection between Gilgamesh and himself than more stories? Shulgi decided to write Gilgamesh's stories down, but he wanted to be in them too; otherwise writing them down would be useless. The whole point of the stories was to give two thumbs way up to Shulgi's kingliness.

So Shulgi squeezed himself into an epic as Gilgamesh's brother, and he changed the curriculum of scribal schools to include poems and hymns praising his own awesomeness. The image wouldn't be complete without an appropriate nickname, and thus Shulgi the Avenger was born, minus any superhero's cape. (Seriously.) He didn't wait till he was dead to have people sing his praises; he commanded it while he was alive, proving just how fuzzy the lines between history and legend can get in the greedy hands of a dictator.

Gilgamesh got the last laugh, though. Shulgi might have used his name and abused his memory for his own purposes, but it's Gilgamesh that people still remember. (Which is a shame, really, since Shulgi was the first to use writing for things other than keeping track of goats and grain—those boring administrative records at work!)

After that, Gilgamesh had a new history—his legend. It was tweaked orally and re-tweaked in writing over and over and over again until we had a bunch of different versions of the story. And like any bestselling novel, *The Epic of Gilgamesh* has been translated into different languages throughout its long history, changing to fit new audiences whom embellished and expanded the old stories. The Babylonians went further; they strung the Sumerian tales together into a cohesive story, added in new story bits (Utnapishtim and the Flood), and upgraded Enkindu's servant status to best friend status.

Before there ever was a *New York Times* bestseller, there was the original: Gilgamesh.

The First at Everything

When you're the world's oldest civilization, it's easy to be the first at everything. The first to read, the first to write, the first to build cities and canals, the first to use a plow, and so on. It comes as no surprise, then, that this ancient Sumerian culture gave us the first epic poetry and the first superhuman character.

Of all the **epics** to come out of Mesopotamia—and there are quite a few—Gilgamesh's are the most widespread and the most copied. They were found all over the present-day Middle East, ranging in date from Shulgi's literary reforms until the second century BCE. That's 1,900 years! It's possible that archaeologists might find even older copies someday.

epics:
Including epics about characters with equally awesome names like Sargon, Lugalbanda, and Etana.

Since the world wasn't isolated in the Bronze Age, even faraway places like Greece and Rome knew about the badly behaving Gilgamesh. Wars, trade routes, migrant workers, travelers, and mercenary jobs all brought these cultures into contact with each other. People did all the sorts of things people do when they get together: shared stories, married, and killed one another. (Isn't that your typical family picnic?) As a result, Gilgamesh and his tales spread far beyond Mesopotamia, influencing *cultures* throughout the known world.

cultures:
Even the monsters in the epic found themselves in the limelight. The epic's forest monster, Huwawa, is also mentioned in the Dead Sea Scrolls and in the medieval work by the Manicheans known as *Book of the Giants.*

The biggest debate between scholars is how much Gilgamesh influenced *One Thousand and One Nights* (a.k.a. *Arabian Nights*) and also Homer (*The Iliad* and *The Odyssey*—see chapter 9).

Achilles, the Greek hero of the Trojan War, and Gilgamesh could be twins, they're so alike. Both are sons of a goddess and king; both are so close to immortality that they could practically taste it; and both are so messed up emotionally, they could be the world's first manic-depressives.

One minute they were weeping bitterly, and the next they were ready to cut off heads and party like it was the end of the world. Both had close buddies who died, forcing them to talk about their feelings, and eventually they both realized that no matter what, death would come for them. Oh well—*carpe diem*! (Which has nothing to do with fish, but with seizing the day.)

narus:

The Near Eastern version of bards—storytelling singers—but can also refer to the type of boast-filled stories about kings that filled tablets.

It's possible that the Greek bards who traveled around various Greek cities singing and performing Greek stories heard Gilgamesh's stories themselves from ***narus***.

They may have even heard the stories from captured soldiers, who were turned into slaves after wars. Maybe they remembered bits of stories and thought, "Perhaps I'll just adjust it a bit for my audience."

There's no reason to assume that the Greek bards straight plagiarized from Eastern traditions, but there's no reason to think they didn't get a bit of inspiration, either. Too many of the same themes, motifs, and characters are present in both traditions. The same thing happens today for writers everywhere. As it's been said: there's nothing new under the sun.

A Merry-Go-Round of Opportunity

Mortality, friendship, and the acceptance of death—these themes can be found in modern books today, but they all began with Gilgamesh.

When Gilgamesh was uncovered in Victorian times, it didn't immediately take the world by storm. At first, only angsty poets, artists, and psychoanalysts—like Sigmund Freud and Carl Jung—salivated while reading about Gilgamesh. Upon reading the epic, the famous Austrian poet Rainer Maria Rilke exclaimed, "Gilgamesch ist unge-heuer!" which means something like, "Gilgamesh is the man!"

It wasn't until after WWII that Gilgamesh managed to infiltrate the rest of the world and capture its attention. Today, Gilgamesh is the star in many media forms, including textbooks, theater, ballet, videogames, novels, comic books, anime, and radio broadcasts. There's even a Gilgamesh-themed restaurant located in London.

All in all, Gilgamesh of the epic tale is fake. It's even possible that Gilgamesh of Uruk is a fraud, too.

Gilgamesh for the People

The Mesopotamian idea of the afterlife was scarier and crueler than a surprise pop quiz on a Friday afternoon. Nothing grew in the Netherworld, and the dead only drank brackish water and ate stale bread. They spent their days hoping the Queen of the Dead, Ereshkigal, didn't notice them moping about and send her demons to punish them. And that was the afterlife for people who had been *good* and obeyed the gods' whims their whole life. It's no wonder Gilgamesh thought dying was a raw deal. His quest for immortality ultimately gave the Mesopotamian people hope. At the end of Gilgamesh's story, the gods grant him a form of immortality—he becomes the greeter of the dead (like Saint Peter in Christian culture) and the judge of the dead (like King Minos in Ancient Greek culture). Gilgamesh's story finally gave Mesopotamians something to look forward to after death—they would be able to meet their hero, the great king!

Scholars just don't know. If he did exist, he wasn't running around for 126 years like the Sumerian King List says he did. But his legacy does exist, and it helped shape Western *and* Eastern literature for centuries. That's some pretty legendary stuff.

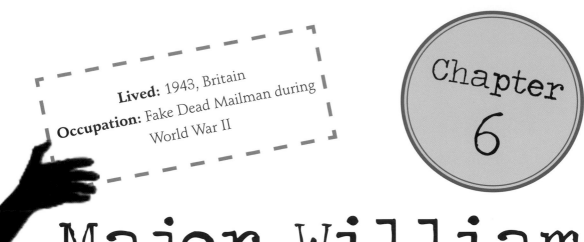

Major William Martin

Operation Mincemeat

Every Good British Spy Story Needs a Little James Bond

No one expected a corpse to change the course of World War II, but then again, no one expected a dead man to be promoted to a major in the British army, either. Desperate times call for desperate measures, and World War II was desperate times.

It was none other than Ian Fleming, creator of James Bond, who helped the Allies invent one crazy (the British would say barmy) deception scheme after another. At the outbreak of war in 1939, Fleming worked as a personal assistant to an admiral. (Hardly a glamorous job for a would-be famous author, but Fleming made the best of it by later turning all of his superiors into characters in his novels.) Together, he and the admiral drafted a top-secret document nicknamed the "Trout Memo," which is a weird name when you think about it. Inside, the dynamic duo listed fifty-one ways to trick the enemy.

As anybody who has ever seen a James Bond movie knows, Ian Fleming had a fertile mind. Today, one might call it an overactive imagination. Most of the ideas in the Trout Memo were too flashy—and others, plain crazy. But one idea in particular, #28, hit just the right note. Appropriately, Ian Fleming entitled it: "A Suggestion (not a very nice one)."

Idea #28 was ambitious and bold. In order for it to work, the British and Americans would need cover stories for their cover stories. They would also need near perfect planning. But if they pulled it off, #28 could change the course of the war. And no one but the Nazis wanted to spend the rest of their lives saying *Heil Hitler*."

Heil Hitler:

Adolf Hitler had a thirst for world domination. He rolled over with tanks, threw in concentration camps, and otherwise killed anyone he didn't like. He really needed to be stopped.

"Everybody But a Bloody Fool Would Know It Was Sicily"

The war wasn't going as well as the Soviet Union, Britain, and America had hoped by 1943. Despite their super catchy, super cool nickname—the Allies—there were still dictators running roughshod all over Europe. The Allies needed to end the war soon, and taking the fight to Hitler's doorstep seemed the best way.

When trying to break a strong chain, it's always best to go for the weakest link. In this case, the weak link was with Hitler's Fascist friend and Italy's dictator, Benito Mussolini. Together with Japan, Hitler and Mussolini were the Axis Powers—another catchy nickname. The Allies wanted to invade Italy first, and to do this, they needed to secure Sicily—that funny-looking island always getting kicked around by Italy's boot.

The Axis Powers used Sicily as a base for German Luftwaffe bombers to launch surprise attacks on the rest of Mediterranean Sea, destroying anything that flew or floated past. It was a real problem, and if Britain and America intended to win the war—and they did—they needed to secure Sicily and smash those death-dealing bombers. The Allies just needed to convince the Axis Powers that they weren't going to do exactly that.

England's Prime Minister, Winston Churchill, even quipped, "Everyone but a bloody fool would know it was Sicily." And even if Hitler and Mussolini were bloody fools, they would catch on rather quickly when 160,000 Allied troops started assembling in that general area. Something like that is hard to miss.

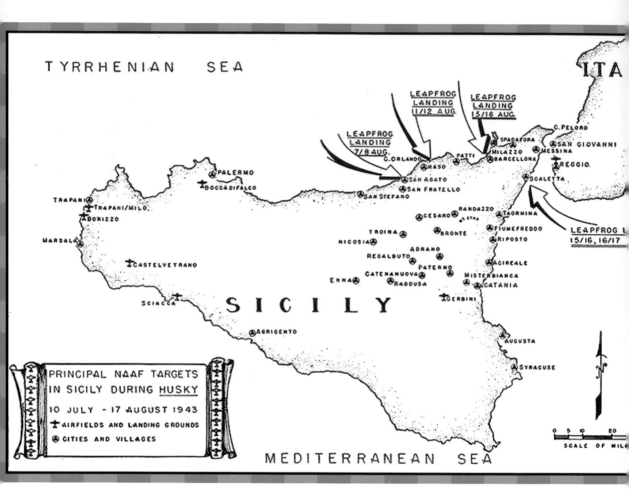

Don't be a bloody fool.

So the British generals realized they needed a daring plan. In order to gain the element of surprise, they needed to pretend their next target wasn't Sicily by pretending that it was Sicily.

Confused yet?

That's where Ewen Montagu entered the story. Despite the fact that his own brother was a Russian spy, Ewen Montague loved his country. He drank his tea, ate his crumpets, and served as a British spy. He also realized that idea #28 would be a perfect fit for the Sicily invasion. Of course, he later claimed that he didn't get the idea from Ian Fleming's memo, but that's all in the past now.

So, what was idea #28, this not very nice suggestion?

Number 28 called for the Allies to use a dead body as a fake spy in order to plant false information in the mind of the enemy. Bogus spies were nothing new in WWII. Legions of fake "sub-agents" roamed Europe, "operating" under the employ of real spies. Having hundreds of fake spies running around distracted the enemy from the real spies, and they also helped validate false information. As you've probably noticed, spying isn't just about stealing secrets or keeping secrets safe. It's also about getting the enemy to believe things that aren't true. That's called **disinformation**, and #28 is a perfect example of that.

disinformation:
Intentionally leaving a false trial.

According to the plan, a corpse would wash up on a beach, presumably after a fiery plane crash in the Atlantic. Attached to the corpse would be documents of a sensitive nature. These top-secret letters—fake, of course— would refer to a plan to invade Greece, but they would also joke about using Sicily as a cover-up.

If the scheme worked, the Germans would get a hold of the letter, re-divert troop strength to Greece, and leave Sicily wide open. Not only that, but the Germans would see any build-up of American and British troops around Sicily

Faker than a $3 bill.

as a trick—as part of the "cover-up" referenced in the letter. That would allow the Allied Powers to prepare for their real attack on Sicily without any suspicion on the enemy's part.

Pretty slick, huh?

As the finishing touch, Ewen Montagu dubbed their plan Operation Mincemeat, since, well, the corpse was kind of like mincemeat pie, minus the flaky crust.

And the Plot Thickens . . .

Before the British could put the plan into action, there were plenty of hurdles to overcome. First, Operation Mincemeat needed a good corpse, which was harder to come by than you'd think during a war where over 60 million people died.

Sure there were lots of bodies—just not the perfect body. The corpse had to be a man who was freshly dead and young. He also had to look like he belonged in the military, but he couldn't have died in combat. They needed the Germans to believe that he had died in a watery plane crash.

autopsy:
Cutting open a body after death to figure out how they died.

Also, he couldn't have any family back home. Mothers typically want those bodies back. A suicide would work—there were plenty of those in Europe during the difficult times of World War II—but most methods, such as ingesting chemicals and hangings, would be discovered during the inevitable *autopsy*.

Luckily for the British, a slightly deranged Welshman named Glyndwr Michael swallowed enough rat poison to kill himself in January 1943. Rat poison, you see, is undetectable in hair samples after death, unlike arsenic and other types of poison. The Germans would never know that's how the man really died.

Ewen Montagu and team put the corpse on ice and began working on the next step in the plan—creating a fictional man to go with the body. He and his staff flipped through their war files and found a name: Major William Martin—a real British pilot. It had a certain ring to it, they decided. They bought the corpse a sharp uniform and took pictures for his ID.

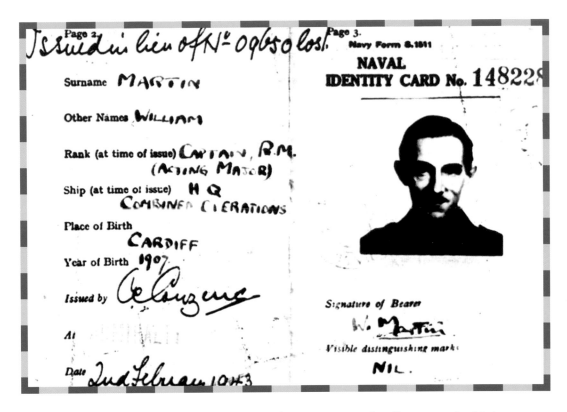

Issued in lieu of N⁰ 09650 lost.

Page 2.

Page 3. Navy Form S.1811

NAVAL IDENTITY CARD No. 148228

Surname **MARTIN**

Other Names **WILLIAM**

Rank (at time of issue) **CAPTAIN, R.M. (ACTING MAJOR)**

Ship (at time of issue) **H Q COMBINED OPERATIONS**

Place of Birth **CARDIFF**

Year of Birth **1907**

Issued by ~~_(signature)_~~

At

Date **2nd February 1943**

Signature of Bearer _W. Martin_

Visible distinguishing marks **NIL.**

Dead men aren't exactly photogenic, so they got a guy in the office to pose for Major Martin's ID card.

Just in case the Germans looked into Major Martin's past, they even made up a fake engagement between him and a real woman and put it in the papers. Luckily for her, she didn't have to go on any real dates with him.

Finally, they assigned the major to the Combined Operations. His new role: to transport the personal letters of Lieutenant General Archibald Nye. Now, it wouldn't look suspicious when the Germans found Nye's letters attached to Martin's arm.

Meanwhile, the real Major Martin didn't have a clue. He spent his days in Rhode Island, teaching the Americans how to fly, which was probably for the best. That way, he'd never hear about his name being used, which he might not be so keen on. Sure, there was the small issue of his death notice, which would probably appear in the local newspapers back in Britain. His friends and family would believe he had died. Maybe they'd even hold a funeral for him. But Ewen Montagu and his team figured they could clear all that up after Operation Mincemeat succeeded. After all, this was war, and sacrifices had to be made.

When Feet Become Popsicles

After all the difficulties finding a suitable corpse, it should have been smooth sailing once one was located. But after three months on ice, the body didn't feel like cooperating. Glyndwr Michael's feet had frozen solid at right angles, which was quite unfortunate when it came time to put on his new boots. Try putting on a boot. The ankle needs to move, but frozen ankles aren't exactly bendy. Montagu's team came up with the idea to defrost just the ankles, slam the boots on, tie them up, and hope the feet didn't fall off. The corpse itself was a little worse for the wear after three months in deep freeze. The eyes had sunken, and the skin had turned yellow. Glyndwr was also skinnier than any British soldier they'd ever seen. But at that point, all they could do was cross their fingers and shove the body in the canister.

Next, Montagu's team set about creating the fake letters that would be found on the body. Montagu didn't waste time agonizing over them. Actually, he quite enjoyed impersonating Nye. It was everyone else that objected. Montagu filled his letters with corny jokes. He found himself hilarious, but everyone else pointed out the obvious—generals don't joke and the Germans had to believe the letter was legit.

After months of countless edits and rewrites, the team finally came up with a solution. They asked Nye himself to write the letter. One would think that a team of creative geniuses would've thought of that earlier, but they were probably overworked and underpaid. As everyone but Montagu suspected, Nye made no jokes. It's probably for the best, since the Germans wouldn't have gotten the jokes anyway.

The letter now had everything it needed including authority. As a finishing touch, the British added a body part to the letter—an eyelash, to be exact. It sounds strange, but the British included one in every letter they sent. Cliché today, but effective during WWII.

Even if the German spies managed to get their hands on a letter and open it, they wouldn't notice the eyelash hanging out in the folds, looking as innocent as a newborn baby. The German spies would re-seal the letter and send it on, thinking they were pretty smooth. Once the Brits got their letter back, that missing eyelash would tell them everything. They'd know that the letter had been read and the information inside compromised.

Now that they had a finished letter and a well-dressed corpse, the team turned to the final problem: where to drop the body? Spain was the obvious choice. Although it was neutral during World War II, it had plenty of German sympathizers and spies that would bring the body to German authorities. The Spanish were also Roman Catholic, meaning they hated autopsies. A few cuts, and they'd be done—nothing too invasive, which was exactly what the Brits wanted.

But Ewen Montagu and his team had to be careful. Spain also had its British sympathizers. What good would it do for the corpse to be handed back to the British with nothing more than a smug grin and a "de nada, amigos"?

Finally, Montagu's team decided to drop the body in the town of Huelva, Spain—a spider's web of German spies and sympathizers. It helped that Germany paid members of the town quite well to keep an eye on British ships passing by on the ocean. That extra cash in the pocket made saying, "Heil Hitler!" a little easier. Thus, the plan was ready to be set into motion.

It's a Go!

Winston Churchill gave the thumbs up, and a date for the drop was set. The Brits even let American General Dwight D. Eisenhower in on the gag, since he ran Allied operations in the Mediterranean.

Montagu's team filled a metal canister with twenty-one pounds of dry ice and stuffed the corpse inside with a bit more dry ice for good measure. Attached to its arm, they chained a briefcase with the fake letters inside. Then, they sealed the canister and put the whole package in a submarine,

The fastest way to deliver a "present" in WWII, including corpses and torpedoes.

Secrets Revealed—Decades Later

The body of Major Martin was buried in Huelva, Spain, shortly after its discovery. For years, the identity of the corpse remained a mystery. Finally, in 1996—over fifty years after Operation Mincemeat—an amateur historian found a document with Glyndwr Michael's name on it. To honor his contribution after death, a small note was added to Major Martin's grave in 1997. It reads: "Glyndwr Michael served as Major William Martin."

What else came out over fifty years later? The commanding officer on board the HMS Seraph "forgot" to mention in his report that he had to use explosives on the canister. In fact, he didn't come clean until 1991.

the HMS *Seraph*. No one but the officers on board knew the canister's actual contents. Most of the sailors thought it was meteorological equipment. A few even used the canister as a pillow. They probably had some weird dreams.

Early in the morning on April 30, the submarine surfaced just outside of Huelva at the drop-off site. The officers pried opened the canister and tried not to puke at the stink. Even though it wasn't part of the plan, they said a quick prayer over the body before pushing it into the water, where it bobbed its way to shore at 4:30 a.m. It all went off without a hitch.

The canister, on the other hand, was a different story. The soldiers needed to sink it in order to hide the evidence, but it refused to go down. Complicating matters, Spanish sardine fisherman were already out, casting their nets in the distance. If they saw a submarine poking out of the water, it would all look pretty suspicious.

The officers considered their options. The sun was coming up and time was running out. They needed to sink that canister! So, they pumped it full of bullets. When that didn't work, they crossed their fingers, threw an explosive in the tank, and dove under water. The bomb maybe lacked finesse, but it was just enough to sink the cargo.

It didn't take long for the body to turn up on shore. One lucky fisherman found it that morning—the explosions and gun shots from the submarine officers probably helped. The British were quickly notified of the dead soldier, but so were the Germans. Now the Brits needed to stall. They had to appear as if they wanted the body back ASAP, but what they really wanted was for the German spies to get there first.

"Mincemeat Was Swallowed Whole"

German spies scrambled to get the briefcase, but unfortunately, it ended up in the hands of the Spanish Navy—and let's just say that the Spanish Navy wasn't a big fan of the Germans. At first, it looked as if the plan had failed, that the Spanish Navy would hand the briefcase right back to the Brits, exactly as Montagu feared. But then, at the last minute, the Spanish government's slow bureaucratic system saved the day—maybe the first and only time *red tape* was a good thing.

red tape: Piles and piles of paperwork.

Due to all the paperwork and forms that had to be filled out for a newly recovered dead body, it took twelve days for the briefcase to get handed back to the British. That delay gave the German spies just enough time to work their magic. They pressured the Spanish to hand over the papers. They got an hour, which was all the time they needed to make copies.

Even better, the documents ended up in the right man's hands—Major Karl-Erich Kühlenthal. Major Kühlenthal was a quarter Jewish, something that could get a man killed in Nazi Germany. So maybe he wanted to impress his Nazi bosses with his great find. Or, maybe he was just a bloody fool. Either way, he didn't question the letters. He personally carried photocopies of everything straight to Germany, where it was just the morale boost Hitler needed after losing Africa.

See, the best way to dupe someone is to use things already in their minds—your enemy's fears and desires. The Germans wanted to believe that they had found top-secret documents, so they did. Anyone who didn't believe the letters kept quiet. Hitler was a dictator, meaning he could pretty much do whatever he wanted, and he wasn't exactly a people person. Good in front of large crowds, yes, but a loose cannon one-on-one. No one wanted to end up on the wrong end of that cannon.

Really, though, things didn't add up and the Germans should have been a bit more skeptical. There were no other bodies found and no wreckage. If the corpse came from a plane crash, how come nothing else had washed ashore?

Plus, the body looked as if it had been dead for months, which it had. But instead of putting the pieces together, the German Intelligence explained it all away. They told themselves that the wreckage sank, that the other bodies were eaten by sharks, and that the sun's rays accelerated the body's decomposition. Anything to make the story make sense.

After Major Kühlenthal made copies, he had the letters expertly resealed and handed back to Spain, but with one minor oversight. There was no eyelash. When the Brits finally got their letters back, they knew that the German's had seen their fake plans. The British authorities sent a telegram to London. It read: "Operation Mincemeat swallowed whole."

Within a month, Hitler transferred much of his power to Greece. He stationed torpedo boats off-shore and built batteries and minefields along the coast. Then his army settled in and waited for the attack.

It never came.

Even after the Allied Powers began their invasion of Sicily, the Germans refused to budge from the Greek shore. Due to Operation Mincemeat, Hitler believed that Sicily was a cover for an even bigger assault on Greece, and he wasn't going to let those crumpet-loving Brits fool him!

How One Fake Spy Can Change a War

Though the invasion of Normandy on D-Day would eventually overshadow it, at the time, Sicily was the largest amphibious landing in the war to date. The Allies came out swinging, striking the enemy on their own land. And thanks to Operation Mincemeat, it went a lot better than it could have. Instead of taking ninety days, as the Allies originally thought, the *offensive* only took thirty-eight. Also, out of the 160,000 Allied men who went into battle, 153,000 survived.

Italy surrendered in September, and its dictator, Benito Mussolini, toppled off his fascist perch.

offensive:

The Allies nicknamed this invasion Operation Husky, which has no connection to Sicily at all—just the way they wanted it.

Even better, Hitler was so embarrassed by the double-cross that he became paranoid. When his spies found real top-secret documents only a few months later, he ignored them, afraid of another Mincemeat debacle.

Of course, Operation Mincemeat didn't single-handedly end the war, but as one well-placed nail in the coffin, it certainly helped. All it took was a real man's name and a dead man's body to create a fake spy who changed the course of the war.

Chapter 7

Lived: Sixteenth century CE, England
Occupation: Actor, Playwright

William Shakespeare

To Be . . . Or Not

Master? Or Monkey . . .

To be or not to be? Shakespeare probably never imagined people asking that question (and one of his most famous lines) about *him*, but then again, maybe he should have. Being the most famous English writer of all time comes with a price. In this case, the price is being called a fraud.

Perhaps it's because when it comes to Shakespeare's real life, there's less to go on than a fake treasure map. Actually, a fake treasure map might be more helpful than what's known about William Shakespeare's life.

What? You thought the most brilliant playwright in history left behind stacks of plays, poems, and letters? You wish. The world doesn't have so much as a couplet in Shakespeare's own hand, only six shaky signatures on legal documents that look as if a trained monkey could've penned them.

No wonder the world's largest literary manhunt turned into a wild goose chase long ago.

That doesn't necessarily mean Shakespeare the play-wright never existed, but you'll have to decide for yourself. Don't worry, there's only about a billion books written on the subject if you want to do some investigative journalism.

Party Like a Rock Star

Shakespeare's story is the stuff of legends, which is maybe why it could be nothing more than one. When does a genius son of a failing glove maker morph from a country kid to a big city hot-shot? And when would he have time along the way to write the

"There's no more faith in thee than in a stewed prune!"
—"Shakespeare's" play, Henry V

greatest plays in the English language and rub elbows with the likes of Queen Elizabeth? Only in the story books.

Let's start at the beginning. Will Shakespeare was born in Stratford-upon-Avon, a small town located about one hundred miles west of London.

His father was a successful merchant. He also held a number of official positions such as the town bailiff—a kind of local mayor. Things started out well for the Shakespeares. They weren't royalty, but they weren't starving either. Then, Will's father got in trouble with the law. He became a dealer of the hottest Elizabethan commodity. Yes, Shakespeare Senior let all that bailiff power go to his head and got into the illegal wool trade, which was a lot riskier, and more dashing, than you'd think. At least, Shakespeare's mom thought so, since she had six kids with Shakespeare Senior.

Shakespeare's birth house oozes sublimity.

grammar school:

Kids started grammar school around age seven in Elizabethan England, where they were taught to read and write, and learn dead languages like Greek and Latin by force.

Getting caught was enough to sink the family's fortunes and force Will to drop out of *grammar school*, probably to help his father make gloves.

At the age of eighteen, William married Anne Hathaway who was twenty-six and pregnant. Today, it could be a reality show, but back then it was just life. Around one-quarter to one-third of all women who got married during this period were already expecting a child when they said, "I do."

Small town life didn't suit Will. Instead of staying home and caring for his wife and three small children, he hitched a ride with a traveling theater company to go play dress-up. Shortly after, Will hit the big time. He produced 39 plays and 150 sonnets. He traveled between Stratford and London, managed a theater company, and was an all-around rock star. He lived the glamorous life, eating caviar and sipping champagne. He was a genius, and luckily for the world, even his poop came out in golden letters.

Eventually, he retired at a ripe old age (his late forties) and died in Stratford on his fifty-second birthday. And the world has loved him ever since.

At least, that's the version we've been led to believe all these years.

Where There's Smoke . . .

There are a lot of problems with the story we've been told about William Shakespeare. First of all, it doesn't make any sense. Running away from home to become an *actor* was not considered okay in 1580s England.

actor: Called a player in those days.

Today, actors are fawned over as celebrities and hounded by the paparazzi, but back then, they were about as cool as a hot steaming pile of horse poo.

Being an actor wasn't even considered a real job. Since they wandered from town to town giving shows, their official occupation was vagrancy, and vagabonds could be arrested, whipped, and branded. This was to ensure that they kept the peace, because who knew when they might break into song and dance—the horror of it! So why would a man give up a respectable trade, like being a glove maker, to become an actor?

The second problem with this story is that it *really* doesn't make sense. (Yes, that's the same as the first reason.) Shakespeare's works display more knowledge than C-3PO's programming. A true Renaissance man, Shakespeare the playwright seems to have an intimate grasp of Elizabethan court life as well as life at foreign courts. His work also shows him to be a master of military terminology, astronomy, mathematics, languages, Classics, law, art, literature, medicine, music, and more.

This poses a big problem—like an eight-hundred-pound gorilla in the room problem—because there's no record of the historical William Shakespeare having attended any school at all, let alone a university. (However, if he actually went, Elizabethan grammar school wasn't like your middle school today. Students either learned their Latin conjugations or it was beat into them with a nice-sized stick.) Although it'd be weird for a bailiff's son not to get some schooling, so most people assume he went for a little while.

So where did all the other learning come from? All that court life know-how had to come from somewhere. Proper bowing techniques and other persnickety protocol wasn't the sort of thing Shakespeare would have been taught in grammar school, and even a genius can't pluck that kind of stuff out of the ether.

There's also no record of Shakespeare ever meeting the queen, living at court, or traveling the world—and this was a time of meticulous record keeping. We have records showing how many times Shakespeare evaded taxes (four times), how many times he tried to sue for petty sums of money (three times), and how many times he was caught hoarding food during a famine (once), but nothing about him meeting Queen Elizabeth. Seems kind of strange, doesn't it?

Perhaps a lot of this could be explained away, like pointing out that Shakespeare's vast knowledge could have come from reading books or that he didn't have to live at court to know its rules. He just had to ask a nobleman a few haughty questions like, "You sir, how dost thou bow?" and he'd know how low to go. One could also argue that he wasn't actually considered a rock star until after he died, so nobody ever thought to save his to-do lists to hawk on eBay.

But the more you dig, the more you realize there are serious problems with each of these explanations. If Shakespeare were self-taught, for example, he would need to have a huge library of books. Where are they, then?

In Shakespeare's will, he details everything he owns, down to his "second-best bed," leaving them all to various people including his wife and fellow players. No books were mentioned anywhere in his will.

Books were expensive possessions back then. If Shakespeare had owned any, he wouldn't have

Lost Years

No one knows what became of the historical William Shakespeare from his twins' birth in 1585 until he pops up again in London in 1592. There's less evidence of what he did during these "lost years" than evidence of Sasquatch. At least there are a few grainy photos of the monster.

For all we know, Shakespeare could have been in Italy, mastering the art of being a gentleman, or traveling the world, becoming savvy in stars (and star-crossed lovers). Maybe he even spent a year in a law office absorbing all that lawyerly wit. But without evidence, that could all just be hogwash. And that's why they're called the "lost years."

forgotten to include them. In fact, there's no mention of him having a literary career at all in his will, and even his name is spelled differently than on his plays, when his name was written at all. One would think he would have wanted to preserve his literary legacy, and having the name "Shakespeare" written down would be the first step. It's all about branding! But does that mean the world has gotten played by the player?

Because we have the plays (which are undeniable) and because so many questions surround the life of the historical William Shakespeare from Stratford-upon-Avon (also undeniable), two camps have formed about his credibility as *the* playwright.

On the one side, there are the Stratfordians, who believe that the historical William Shakespeare from Stratford-upon-Avon wrote Shakespeare's plays. On the other side, there are the Anti-Stratfordians. These individuals believe that a man named William Shakespeare existed, but that he wasn't the self-taught genius of legend. The Anti-Stratfordians think he was an actor, possibly half-witted, and the front man for the real writer of the greatest plays in the English language.

How did all this doubt start?

Fighting words in Elizabethan times: "Your brain is as dry as the remainder biscuit after voyage."
—"Shakespeare's play, As You Like It

. . . There's Usually a Fire

It wasn't until the literary world made Shakespeare out to be the English god of really good writing that anyone took a step back and scratched their thick beards.

See, a contagious idea called *bardolatry* spread through the nineteenth century as quickly as the plague spread through the sixteenth century. This was the time in which Shakespeare became a god. Literary snobs who worshipped Shakespeare's plays knew they were deeper than the ocean. Obviously, they must have been written for the high-class thinkers (like themselves). So instead of remembering his true origins, people began to worship him as the most intelligent human being to ever grace the earth.

From Bear-Baiting to Theater-Going

Despite the inherent snootiness that comes to mind when you think of Shakespeare's plays, they were pretty much the opposite in Elizabethan England. People didn't break out their furs and monocles to go to the theater in Shakespeare's day. Instead, they filled their pockets with rotten fruit and their bellies with beer. Then they stood jowl-to-jowl, hooting and hollering throughout the performance.

Shakespeare's plays competed with bear baiting for its audience, which wasn't exactly highbrow entertainment. In bear baiting, a bear was chained to the ground while dogs attacked it. As the dogs died, a new one replaced it until the bear died or people ran out of dogs.

Nobles also attended plays back then, but they sat above the riffraff. Thus, playwrights had to write stories that appealed to both classes. Shakespeare's theater company, the King's Men, was able to do both. That's why they thrived in the common theaters like the Curtain and the Globe, and were also invited for special performances at Whitehall for royal eyes and ears.

Then, a guy named Samuel Mosheim Schmucker brought that house of cards tumbling down—accidently. Schmucker didn't like the way people had begun to doubt the existence of Jesus Christ, so in 1848, he wrote a book. He aimed to show everyone just how very foolish it was to doubt a man's existence just because he was born to a poor, lower class family, had little formal education, and left behind no historical records. Look at Shakespeare! He only left behind legal documents, but he was still a god of writing.

Schmucker's plan backfired. Instead of convincing people that Jesus was real, people started questioning Shakespeare's existence, too. Whoops.

Now that Shakespeare's existence was called into question, those snobby elites remembered something else. The bard known as Shakespeare never went to Oxford or Cambridge—or anywhere else associated with higher learning—and the backlash began. Poor Shakespeare went from being dead, to being a near-god, to never existing in the course of a few decades. People started wondering how a self-educated son of a glove maker penned the greatest works of the English language when his signatures showed his writing wasn't exactly "Shakespeare."

The first alternative candidate to be proposed as the real Shakespeare was none other than Sir Francis Bacon, inventor of the scientific method. Leading the Baconian charge was a woman named Delia Bacon. (No relation.)

With the help of illustrious friends like Ralph Waldo Emerson, Nathaniel Hawthorne, and Samuel Morse (inventor of the Morse code), Delia Bacon traveled from America to England, determined to dig up the grave of Shakespeare. She wasn't hoping to find just the bard's bones, but secret documents proving the man was a fake.

She lost her nerve and never dug up a corpse. Even though she wasn't able to prove her hypothesis, she was still the first to throw out the revolutionary idea that Shakespeare was actually a group of writers all helping pen the plays with Sir Francis Bacon as the lead writer.

devastated:
She also convinced herself along the way she must have been related to the great thinker, Sir Francis Bacon. She wasn't.

Everyone hated it. At least, at first. Unfortunately for Delia, no one really took her seriously until after her death. She died in an insane asylum, two years after the publication, *devastated*.

Shakespeare's ghost sighed in relief and rolled back over in his grave, undisturbed. But he wasn't out of the woods yet.

Whodunnit?

It's possible the esteemed author of such masterfully witty phrases as, "More of your conversation would infect my brain," couldn't write a sentence, let alone some of the greatest insults ever thrown at another person. But someone had to come up with lines such as, "Methink'st thou art a general offense and every man should beat thee." So who did?

At last count, seventy-seven candidates have been in the running for the real William Shakespeare.

Of course, in order to dethrone the king of playwrights there had to be more evidence than Shakespeare's simple lack of education. So the manhunt began.

Since doubters convinced themselves it had to be a court insider, everyone started looking for a nobleman. Sir Francis Bacon was the first, but he wasn't the last. It got pretty easy to see clues in every mundane detail the deeper into conspiracy theories people sank. They hunted through Shakespeare's plays to find clues and cryptograms regarding the true author, and they came up with wild answer after wild answer.

By looking hard enough, some started to think the playwright was none other than Queen Elizabeth, herself. Maybe she used William Shakespeare as her face to the world, since she was a girl and girls weren't allowed to publish plays. Especially if that girl was queen and the plays were for the common masses. It might sound crazy, but people like crazy. (For the record, it wasn't the queen.)

More modern literary analysis (i.e., not simply digging up graves) studies patterns in the writings using computer programs. This way, scholars can pretend they're CSI detectives. They look at things like repeated words and phrases in all Elizabethan works. Even the classical blunders in Shakespeare are used to prove that the man from Stratford didn't need a college education to write the plays. In fact, it would make more sense if he didn't have any university learning.

These experts also trace the development of the writing over the years as Shakespeare matured. Then, they compare it to the known writings from other candidates to compare writing tics, peculiar words, spelling patterns, and the handwriting itself. All of these linguistic (language) patterns act like fingerprints to help ID authors instead of bad guys.

These methods have allowed scholars to discover a number of things about Shakespeare's plays. First, if some of the handwritten manuscripts are really Shakespeare's, he had worse penmanship than a preschooler. But you already knew that from his signatures.

Second, at least five of the plays were co-written, but it may be many more. Like most playwrights working for theater houses of the time, Shakespeare didn't write alone. He collaborated with actors and writers, hoping to beat out the other theater houses for best attendance. To do that, he needed lots of plays oozing with dirty jokes and potty humor. Even a genius can only come up with so many fart jokes and stinging insults, so he had lots of help from fellow bawdy players.

Third, almost all of Shakespeare's plays came from an earlier source. Elizabethan writers wouldn't call it plagiarizing back then and adapting older stories for a modern audience is nothing new. Everyone did it.

Shakespeare's most famous play—*The Most Excellent and Lamentable Tragedie of Romeo and Juliet*—was borrowed. Fellow Englishman, Arthur Brooke, published a poem titled *The Tragicall Historye of Romeus and Juliet* in 1562.

Brooke's version wasn't even the first. There's an older Italian version of the star-crossed lovers' story. Clearly, this tale about doomed teenage love had been kicking around Europe for quite some time before Shakespeare added his own flair.

Besides tweaking some names and adding enough suspense to make Hollywood sob with joy, Shakespeare also transformed the moral aspect of the Romeo and Juliet story. Arthur Brooke's characters were "a couple of unfortunate lovers thralling themselves to unhonest desire, neglecting authority and advice of parents and friends." In other words, they wind up dying because they're young and stupid.

But for romantic Shakespeare, that ending simply wouldn't do. He made Romeo and Juliet a "pair of star-crossed lovers" whose tragic deaths end their parents' constant fighting.

That's one for true love, but the real winner is the Grim Reaper. He gets his victims in both versions.

True love at first sight: 1. Grim Reaper: 2.

A little help here?

(It does say tragedy in both titles, after all.)

So forget what you think about Shakespeare making up all those devastatingly romantic tragedies. He wasn't the first, and he won't be the last.

Fame Game

Who doesn't love a good scandal? A man who, for hundreds of years, parades around as the best playwright and poet in the Western world pretty much tops the list of good scandals. If it's true—and William Shakespeare really was just a small town boy who became an actor and nothing more—then William Shakespeare the writer was more phony than baloney. He could've been a pen name for any number of noblemen (or noblewomen) but he wasn't the man we learn about and revere today.

On the other hand, maybe he did exist as William Shakespeare the writer, but not as the single genius slaving over quill and parchment, straining his eyes by candlelight. Maybe "Shakespeare" was a pen name for a collaborative set of writers trying to make a shilling or two off their witty wordplay.

The debate will rage on, but as Charles Dickens once said, "The life of Shakespeare is a fine mystery, and I tremble everyday lest something should come out." In other words, maybe the mystery is the best part of William Shakespeare.

Or perhaps the mystery of the famous bard is really just a warning: Don't get too famous, or in another five hundred years, everyone might wonder if you ever existed.

Pick Your Camp

When it comes to who produced Shakespeare's work, the sides don't just break down into Strafordian or Anti-Stratfordian camps. It's way more complicated than that. Baconians are Anti-Stratfordians who believe Sir Francis Bacon wrote Shakespeare. Oxfordians believe it was Edward de Vere, the Seventeenth Earl of Oxford. Currently, Oxford is the top candidate and here's why:

- He had classical training, a lawyer background, and the court know-how so resplendent in Shakespeare's works.
- He was known as a writer by his contemporaries.
- He traveled all over Italy, where thirteen of Shakespeare's plays are set.
- The plays seem to follow his life.
- Oxford's family has links to the publication of Shakespeare's First Folio, a collection of thirty-six plays printed after Shakespeare's (and Oxford's) death.

If that doesn't convince you, then you probably don't believe in Sasquatch, either.

Chapter 8

"**Occupation**": Pope
"**Lived**": England, Germany, Greece, Italy

Pope Joan

Not to be Confused with Pope John I-XXIII

A Letter Off

One day in the Middle Ages— the year 855 CE—Pope John was riding a horse to St. Peter's Basilica in Rome. Whenever the pope went anywhere he was surrounded by lots of people who wanted to be close to his Holiness. That was usually a good thing. It meant he was loved and adored. But on this occasion, it was bad news for Pope John. Very bad news. That's because the Holy Father was actually a holy mother— the world just didn't know it yet. Yes, Pope John was really Pope Joan.

As soon as everyone realized the pope was a woman AND giving birth in broad daylight, they got so angry at being duped that they started throwing stones at her. Literal ones and probably pretty big ones, too, because they ended up *stoning* Pope Joan and the baby to death. Not a pretty sight.

stoning:

There's a nicer version of the story that claims Pope Joan was whisked away to a nunnery and allowed to raise her son there, but most accounts prefer the gruesome ending.

You probably have a lot of questions right now. The biggest one is: How the heck did a woman ever get elected pope in the first place? Women aren't allowed to be priests, let alone cardinals, bishops, and popes! Or, perhaps you're wondering if the whole story was a fake, and if so, who started it?

You're not alone. People have been talking about Pope Joan for centuries. They've debated her existence, tried to silence her story, and used her as a poster child of a corrupt church. What's weird is nobody talked about a Pope Joan until hundreds of years after her unfortunate demise. It was as if nobody found the story strange. Then they couldn't stop talking about her.

The Evidence

The first mention of Pope Joan comes from a Catholic source. According to Jean de Mailly, a Dominican friar writing around 1250, a really smart woman decided an endless life of mind-numbing chores and back-breaking drudgery in a mud hut didn't suit her. She was too clever to spend all day hefting sacks of cow poo over her back and fertilizing gardens.

So she did something about it. She cut her hair, dressed as a monk, and went to study in Italy. Since she was so smart, she worked her way up the papal ladder until she was unanimously voted in as pope around 1100. De Mailly's account ends with Pope Joan getting stoned to death. He also ended it with a caution, saying he doubts the truth of the legend and that someone should really look into it.

This story didn't make any tsunami-like waves in the Catholic Church—or even a watery ripple—probably because, in 1250, the only people reading de Mailly's chronicle were other monks. But then, years later, another Dominican writer found the legend of Pope Joan. Martinus Polonus must have liked the sound of a popess because he took the story and ran with it, giving the woman a name, fleshing out her backstory, and even adding a motive to the crime—ooey, gooey love. (You know what they say. Give a medieval monk an inch and he takes a mile.) His version became *the* version of Pope Joan and everyone excitedly *copied* it.

copied:
This was back when if you wanted to publish a story, you had to write it out by hand under dim candlelight—each and every copy.

According to Polonus, the woman's name was Johannes, but she went by John of Mainz. She disguised herself as a monk in order to go traveling and studying in Athens with a boy, but ended up delighting all of her teachers with her exceptional brain once there. Then she went to Rome. It didn't take long for everyone to realize "John" should become the next pope. Polonus thought she was elected around 853, so the dates are different from de Mailly's account, but the ending is still the same—Pope Joan gives birth and dies under an onslaught of rocks.

Once again, no tsunamis of protest spewed from Polonus's account. Why was this? Shouldn't a cross-dressing, lying, female pope be what you'd call "a problem" for the Church?

Not really. At least, not at first. The fact that a woman dressed as a man and got away with it wasn't really an issue. That kind of thing happened more often than you'd think. It was easier to do at a time when people didn't bathe as much and wore baggy linens for clothing. Monks' outfits were even better for hiding womanly parts. Their potato sack couture covered everything, even delicate little wrists.

Actually, it might not be too difficult to keep the jig going—until death, at least. There are around twenty different male saints who ended up being

Someone call the fashion police!

women. No one knew until they died and started washing the body for burial. (Except for the most famous cross-dressing saint of all time—Saint Joan of Arc. She didn't pretend to be a man. She just dressed like one, since riding a horse is easier in pants than a dress.) All twenty of them still got to be saints.

If a Girl Could Do It . . .

Even before the Protestant Revolution, people used the story of Pope Joan to criticize the Catholic Church. Here are two of the more famous critics:

Giovanni Boccaccio: an Italian humanist. Yes, Boccaccio was certainly human, but that's not what a humanist is. Instead of focusing on religious stuff, humanists focused on the humanities: logic, grammar, history, and so on. Boccaccio is best known for the *Decameron*, a series of poems and tales, but he also wrote about Pope Joan. He put her among his "most famous women in history" book, *De Claris Mulieribus* (published in 1374). For Boccaccio, it wasn't a question of whether Pope Joan actually existed. She clearly did. It was more of a question of the Church allowing bad leaders to take charge all the time. To Boccaccio, they needed some serious help. As for her death, he doesn't mention it. He says a bunch of cardinals (not birds, but priests) put her behind bars for the rest of her life so she could think about what she did—that wicked woman.

John Hus: a Bohemian reformer. Hus really didn't like the pope, but there weren't a lot of options for changing religions in medieval Europe. So, instead, he wrote a bunch of angry letters stating things like *the Church was perfectly capable of functioning without a pope. Look at all the times when a false pope was on the throne, like that woman, Joan.* This didn't exactly make him popular with the pope, who had John burned at the stake in 1415.

So this sort of thing happened, and everyone went on with their lives. Throughout the fifteenth century, no one doubted the story of Pope Joan, and no one much cared.

A few people used the story of the female pope to attack the current pope, but even then, her existence wasn't a big deal.

She was even mentioned in a medieval guidebook from 1375 so interested travelers could visit the site of her stoning near the Colosseum, and search for blood-stained souvenirs. After the sixteenth century, Catholics everywhere decided the story was fake and denied it like mad. So, what gives?

One word: Protestants.

Collateral Damage

In 1517, Martin Luther, a soon-to-be fugitive, tacked to a church door ninety-five reasons why he felt the Catholic Church's rules stunk and ways to make them stink a little less. Long story short, the Church didn't appreciate his suggestions and *excommunicated* him.

Luther didn't go down easy. Or alone. He brought lots of unhappy Catholics with him, and this split led to a new sect of Christianity: Protestantism. It wasn't an easy or happy split. In fact, it was it was even more sad than a banana split with no bananas, and it led to hundreds of years of name calling and bloody wars.

excommunicated:
They kicked him out for good.

After the Church split into Catholics and Protestants, Pope Joan wasn't the black sheep of the family anymore, or even just some embarrassing rumor. She became a sheep in both sides' cross-hairs.

Protestants were positively giddy to come across the old story of a female pope. To them, it showed why the papacy had to go—it had become a sad joke. In the eyes of the Protestants, Pope Joan proved that Catholics were so corrupt that they had thrown all their traditions down the toilet, which in sixteenth-century Europe was usually a hole in the ground (cesspit) or a box with a lid for fancy folks.

To really drive the point home, Protestants turned Pope Joan into a sorceress, a necromancer, a demon, and a pawn of the Devil. There was no way a woman could be that smart! She must have signed her soul to the Devil in exchange for a brain. And the Catholics were too corrupt to see it happening or to stop it.

To be fair, this happened with male popes who were brighter than the average candle, too. Pope Sylvester II (pope from 999 to 1003) was also accused of signing away his soul to the devil, so it didn't always pay to be smarter than everyone else in medieval Europe. Suddenly you got accused of inking block-buster deals with the devil.

With all this hostility, there was only one thing the Catholic Church could do—play Peter and thrice deny. In 1562, an Augustinian friar set out to disprove all the Pope Joan stories. Soon, the whole Church backtracked, saying this story about a popess was nothing more than Protestant drivel. Then they tried to wipe out all traces of her. This included getting rid of any statues of her, like the one in the Siena Cathedral in Italy. Pope Clement VIII had

Aristotle Was Here!

Graffiti is very common today, but it isn't a modern invention. People love to scribble their mark on the world. There's graffiti from ancient times making fun of Julius Caesar, and there's graffiti from medieval times in manuscripts. One manuscript has graffiti in the margins that states: "The Pope was a woman." Now, clearly this sounds like something a sassy Protestant would scribble in a Catholic book, but when scientists tested the ink, they found it was older than Protestantism. Only a Catholic could have done it. So much for denial!

Protestant Reformation:

It started with Martin Luther in 1517 and ended in 1648 after a long, bloody war called The Thirty Years' War—no points for imagination. By the time the war was over, people had forgotten what they were fighting about.

it re-carved into a different pope in 1600—and he made sure it was a male one.

Protestants didn't let the matter go that quietly, however. During the *Protestant Reformation*, Pope Joan had hundreds of pamphlets written about her. It was an all-out smear campaign. Just because there's a lot of stuff written about her, though, doesn't mean she was real. It means people liked the *idea* of her. The only thing the Catholics could do was feign ignorance—who, us? And this leads to the big question: Why did they create a story about a woman pope in the first place?

Scared of a Girl

Back in the thirteenth century, when Jean de Mailly and Martinus Polonus lived, women started to want new things for themselves. Not shoes or purses, but positions of power in the Church. They could be just as religious as men, they insisted, so why couldn't they be leaders, too? Why couldn't they hear confessions and touch religious vessels? Women wanted to be priests and they wanted a chance at an education. It was a mini-renaissance in the thirteenth century, and it scared the mitre caps right off the men in charge.

This was also the time when a lot of cross-dressing happened. Women dressed as men so they could learn. The male priests didn't like this, but there was one thing they didn't like even more.

Large numbers of women were forming their own religious communities and they weren't consulting any men first. These independent women were called **beguines**, and they didn't need a man telling them what to do.

To priests, this was even worse than the large number of women trying to get into the man-approved convents! Eventually, in 1312, the Council of Vienna outlawed the beguines and married them all off.

This political background explains one of the most popular theories about the source of the Pope Joan story. At a time when women were gaining more religious

How about a sparkly pair of shoes instead?

authority, some think that it was invented as a cautionary tale to help keep women in check. Look what happens when women try to be priests—they give birth, which is kind of a deal breaker. According to priests, you can't be thinking about God if you're having a baby.

Another theory involves politics of a different kind. Some think the story of Pope Joan started because the Dominican authors wanted the popes at the time to stop acting like spoiled brats and start behaving themselves. (Obviously, those popes took power away from the Dominican priests ASAP.)

> **beguines:**
> Religious women who weren't nuns. They formed a girl's only clubhouse and made up all their own rules about worshiping and religion.

By pointing out that a woman was allowed to hold the highest position in the Catholic Church, the priest showed that mistakes happen even at the highest level. If a woman could become pope, so could a wicked man. (Hint, hint, he seemed to be saying. There might be a wicked man on the papal throne right now.)

Even if that wasn't the source of the Pope Joan story, it was used that way. In 1332, a Franciscan friar, William of Ockham, went to a lot of trouble connecting the dots between Pope Joan and the current corrupt pope. The point of his exercise: if God allowed a false pope to be in charge once, he could do it again.

In either case, both possibilities highlight what men thought about women at the time, and it wasn't very nice.

Knocking on Wood

Whether or not Pope Joan's story was true (doubtful), superstitions surrounding it stuck with people. Some Italian families liked the story of a popess so much that they had their tarot card decks include Pope Joan as the trump card.

Trump that!

Popes in the fifteenth century always took a detour around the road where Pope Joan supposedly gave birth, although it wasn't certain if she existed and therefore had a child. Even the street was named after her, Vicus Papissa. One pope, Innocent VIII, got in trouble for refusing to avoid the intersection. Popes don't avoid it now, but that may be because the street was widened in the seventeenth century and their processions can actually fit down it today.

Another tradition stated that the prospective pope had to sit on a throne with a hole in it before becoming pope. A lowly deacon felt around, made sure the new guy had the goods, and declared to the world that the pope was indeed a man (just in case a cross-dressing woman ever tried that stunt again). This doesn't happen today, if it even happened in the past.

Pope Joan was never meant to be fawned over and admired. She was too scary for that. Instead of illustrating that women can successfully hold power, the story of Pope Joan showed what happens when weak men were in charge—they let women grab their power. It also "proved" that intelligent women were dangerous, since they were probably in league with the Devil to get that smart in the first place. Thus, it became common practice to keep women locked away in the nunneries and the kitchens so they couldn't test out their smarts.

Yet to this day, modern women look to Pope Joan to prove how far a smart woman can go—all the way to the top. Martinus Polonus said in his narrative that Joan was a successful pope until she gave birth. Some Protestant writers claimed that she was a better pope than all those really bad male ones—like the ones who had hordes of illegitimate kids or lived like kings instead of priests.

Pope Joan continues to be a twenty-first-century icon symbolizing what women could accomplish in the Church in the Middle Ages and beyond. Pope Joan really can't be much more than that today since her story is just that—a story.

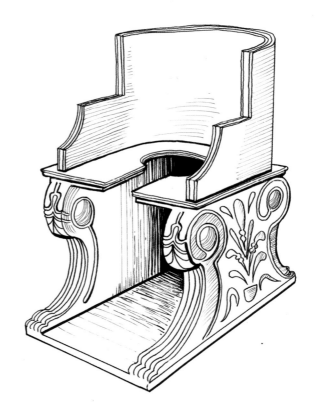

Just checking . . .

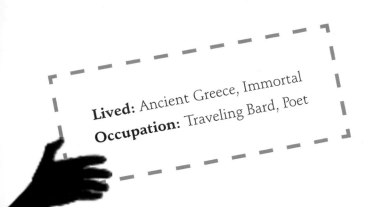

Lived: Ancient Greece, Immortal
Occupation: Traveling Bard, Poet

Chapter
9

Homer

Blind Bard Be Nimble

Cooler Than a Zombie

Homer is kind of like a zombie. No matter how many times you kill him, he always comes back. Maybe that's because studying Homer has been a thing since ancient times, and all signs indicate that won't change. Just to be clear, we're not talking about Homer Simpson of donuts and *d'oh*, but Homer of gods and men and really long stories.

The legend of Homer is too good to pass up. People love it. A blind bard travels throughout Greece reciting poetry to the masses. Along the way, he single-handedly pens two of the greatest stories in Western culture, *The Iliad* and *The Odyssey*, establishing the basis for all literature to follow.

Unfortunately, almost none of it is true.

The epics themselves exist. The Ancient Greeks heard them recited at events like public festivals and private funerals. At some point, Homer's poems made the leap from mouth to papyrus. From there, the stories were copied more times than knockoff Gucci bags. Alas, Homer, himself, did not exist.

Yes, it's true. He was faker than a beauty queen's smile.

Warning! Spoilers Ahead

Greek epics may start out as historical events with real people and real heroes, but over time, these truths were treated more like LEGO bricks. They were used as the building blocks to create new stories and scenes wherever they went.

Our versions of *The Iliad* and *The Odyssey* reflect the time in they were written down—Archaic Greece, circa 750 BCE—but with lots of echoes from centuries past. In those times, men were farmers and herders, and they did manly things like raiding other cattle herds and going to war.

Battlefield reporter, he was not.

Greece was dusting itself off from its own Dark Ages in the eighth century BCE. For the last few hundred years, people in the Mediterranean were mostly huddled together in small communities, just trying to survive. Art, writing, and other time-wasting pursuits weren't exactly high priority compared to eating. Then suddenly . . . two fully-formed epics popped out of nowhere. What the Zeus was going on in Greece?

Well, it was the best of times; it was the worst of times; it was the age of wisdom; it was the age of foolishness . . . wait, wrong story. This story, *The Iliad*, is about wrath. All twenty-four books of it.

The Iliad tells the story of Agamemnon and Achilles, the original mean girls, except they were guys. Despite being on the same side in the Trojan War, these two couldn't even pretend to like each other. Both were fighting the Trojans in the name of honor, which was a big deal in Ancient Greece and people had no problem dying to preserve it.

Agamemnon's kid brother, Menelaus of Sparta, had his wife stolen by Prince Paris of Troy. (Paris wasn't a girl's name back then.) Menelaus couldn't let this slight go unanswered. He had to get his honor and his wife, **Helen**, back.

Helen:

Yes, this is the story of the beautiful Helen of Troy, who was originally Helen of Sparta and then, *spoiler alert* Helen of Sparta at the end.

Menelaus and Agamemnon talked Achilles, the greatest warrior in Greece, into helping them batter down the doors of Troy, because they heard they couldn't do it without him. The only problem: Achilles didn't take directions very well. Or criticism, or insults, or anything but praise. And that's not exactly the recipe for a good soldier.

Throughout the Trojan War, Achilles and Agamemnon did little things to show how much they despised each other, which included stealing girlfriends and calling each other names. It didn't degenerate into hair pulling, but it might as well have. Finally, Achilles got so angry that he refused to fight anymore—which was a problem, since *The Iliad* is sort of his story. He's called the best of the Greeks, multiple times, for good reason. He didn't look very great, moping in his tent for the first nine books of the story though.

See, Achilles knew his way around a sword. Being the son of a goddess helped in the muscle department, of which Achilles had a lot. But being a mama's boy hindered him in the people skills department. Instead of raising Cain on the wife-stealing Trojans, he raised his voice to the gods, whining about the girlfriend-stealing Agamemnon.

With Achilles no longer willing to fight, the Greeks knew they had no chance at victory. Morale was sagging until Achilles's best friend, Patroclus, decided to take matters into his own hands. He put on Achilles's armor and rallied the Greek troops. Everyone got really excited, except for the Trojans, of course. They weren't so thrilled.

Patroclus was no Achilles. Sure, he was good, but in the end, he still got himself killed by Hector, Troy's best warrior. Patroclus's death finally snapped Achilles out of his temper tantrum. He put aside his petty dislike of Agamemnon and joined the battle, just so he could exact revenge on Hector by killing and decimating his corpse. In Ancient Greece, this was a bigger insult than a "yo mamma" joke. It was an insult to end all insults!

In the end, it all worked out for Agamemnon. During a battle, Achilles got shot in the heel, his only weak spot. (Hence the tendon near our ankle being called our Achilles tendon.) Achilles died on the battlefield, and Odysseus thought up the Trojan Horse scenario to sneak inside the walls. Helen went back to Sparta, and Agamemnon went home triumphant (where his wife promptly killed him, but that's another story).

For the Greeks, *The Iliad*—with all its honor and killing and revenge—was pure gold. They knew they had a hit on their hands, so they decided to make a sequel of sorts—*The Odyssey*.

The Odyssey tells the story of that wily coyote, Odysseus, who left the battle of Troy with over six hundred of his men. After the ten-year Trojan War, everyone was ready to get home to Ithaca, but it didn't take long for them to all buy the farm (that means "to die"). What started out as a few days journey at sea turned into another ten years' struggle to get home. That's not as catchy as a three-hour tour, like *Gilligan's Island*, but it's way more adventurous.

While Odysseus's men were smashed to bits, drowned, or eaten alive one monstrous mouthful at a time, he survived thanks to his cunning and his intelligence (and the gods). There was one god, the sea god Poseidon, who'd rather see Odysseus sleeping with the fishes (another way to say "dead"), but he was overruled.

In between all that adventure, Homer cuts to Odysseus's wife and child back home. Despite twenty years, his wife, Penelope, has stayed faithful and kept the kingdom running in his absence. But when men see a single woman with a kingdom attached, they typically try to get a piece of the pie. Soon, Penelope had suitors coming out of her ears, eating all her food and generally being irritating.

But this story has a happy ending. For Odysseus, anyway. He finally got home, reconnected with his son, and together they bathed in a warm blood bath of suitors to secure his kingdom.

All's well that ends well.

How to Avoid Rotten Tomatoes

Those were the mini versions of *The Iliad* and *The Odyssey*. In the hands of a professional, the stories could last for days. Yes, days. Instead of television, people would listen to professional singers, or bards, recite epic tales. Homer calls these early singers *aoidoi*.

Performing one of these stories was a colossal task that required a man and a musical instrument to stand in front of a crowd and sing. (And yes, they were all men, these *aoidoi*. For all that talk about the Greeks inventing democracy, they didn't have the most progressive society.)

The crowds would gather around the bard as if they were at a rock concert. If someone wanted to throw a rotten tomato at the guitarist/lyre-player for

Close enough to smell them sweat. Ancient odeon in Ephesus, Turkey.

flubbing a chord, they didn't have to have good aim. It paid to be flexible, and not just for ducking rotten fruit.

If an audience began to get restless, a bard would simply switch gears and invent a new line or tweak an old line of the story. Of course, these bards weren't dummies. Their new version would sing the praises of their listeners, and the bard would make them feel special by showing how their city was particularly brave or how it had sent more men with Agamemnon than any other.

A bard didn't memorize every line of an epic poem. He used a basic structure of repetitions, plots, and themes to help guide him. The epics had a vast numbers of lines to remember—over 25,000—which explains why it took days to complete. It was also easier to remember the same few names for Achilles, that *swift-footed stud*, than making up an awesome new one every time.

swift-footed stud:

Called "epithets," these repetitious nicknames helped singers plug in something familiar and gave them more time to think of the next line. Swift-footed Achilles was always popular.

This basic structure of the story acted as a road map, and it gave the bard something familiar to toss into his performance while he thought of his next line—a cool line, a line that would keep him from getting hit in the head with a rotten tomato. Because let's face it, memorizing days-upon-days-worth of story isn't fun for anybody.

As a result, *The Iliad* and *The Odyssey* weren't fixed stories; they were more like Jell-O. They could wiggle a lot, but still keep their overall form. These *aoidoi* were the real creative forces behind the details and drama of each epic tale.

In later centuries, performers looking for fame and fortune—called *rhapsodes*—recited these stories at big festivals. Their name literally means "stitchers of songs." They sewed all the different versions together to create their own according to their tastes and talents. Poor *rhapsodes* didn't get a musical accompaniment during their competitions, though—they recited alone and crossed their fingers that their voices didn't break.

Because of this oral tradition, there were probably a lot of different versions of the stories floating around the ancient world. Audience pressure, current

A rhapsode in action, which means a lot of staff leaning.

events, and changing values all helped shape the Homeric epics as they were told and retold for hundreds of years. In fact, the oldest papyrus fragments from the second century BCE contain different lines from our modern edition of Homer's epics. That's six hundred years after the first supposed written copy.

We have no idea how much our versions vary from the original performances of these stories. And we never will, unless someone invents a time machine. Fingers crossed.

Like a Roach

It's clear that both *The Iliad* and *The Odyssey* stem from oral tradition and that they existed before writing. Homer lurks in there somewhere, but where is anyone's guess.

All that genius coming from one man made even the Ancient Greeks a little suspicious. Everyone from Socrates to Plato debated his existence. That didn't mean the Greeks didn't love him, because they did. At least seven places tried to claim their city as his birthplace.

To the Greeks, Homer was the best and greatest poet, the father of all literature. To early scholars, it seemed one minute the Greeks were living in the Dark Ages, just trying to survive, and the next, two fully-formed epics **sprang** out of the universe, perfect in every way.

sprang:
Early scholars of Homeric poetry even started calling him The Big Bang of Western literature. They didn't know about poor, forgotten Gilgamesh—see chapter 5.

But now you know the truth: oral transmission through centuries of singers and performances helped shape those epics. Not some blind guy with a reed pen following Achilles around asking for his autograph.

And the Award for Craziest Theory Goes To . . .

Because Ancient Greece existed a long time ago (hence the *ancient* part), it's hard to figure out exactly what happened during the Trojan War, and if it's at all like *The Iliad* shows it. Nobody knows who Homer was or when exactly *The Iliad* and *The Odyssey* were created, but that doesn't stop people from coming up with some pretty interesting theories. Here are a couple of them.

Co-evolution

This theory claims that the stories evolved with something else—in this case, it's the alphabet.

The Phoenicians, the Greeks' neighbors, brought the royal color purple, their gods, and luxury goods like ivory to Greece. Arguably, the Greeks had all these things before, but the Phoenicians had a certain *Je ne sais quoi.* They made them look so much better. The Greeks couldn't help but trade with the Phoenicians and, as a result, they came into contact with a little something called the alphabet.

Sure it didn't look like our alphabet today; it was missing a few letters. You'd call them vowels, which seems important today, since all the cool words need vowels.

Some scholars believe the Greeks loved the oral versions of Homer so much that they developed their own version of the Phoenician alphabet, vowels included, in order to write them down. In other words, Homer's stories and the Greek alphabet co-evolved together.

That may or may not be the truth, but it's definitely true that the earliest the poems could be from is the Archaic period—when the Greeks started trading with the Phoenicians and found the alphabet.

> **Je ne sais quoi:**
> French for: "I don't know what." Usually a special "I don't know what." The Phoenicians had flair, and the Greeks liked what they saw.

Crystallization

According to this theory, the stories were retold over and over until they settled into their current version and were written down then.

Some scholars think the epics crystallized in Athens, since Athens was a center of learning in Ancient Greece. And during the Classical period—480 to 323 BCE—Athens was the belle of the ball. The Persian Wars ended, and life was good (unless you were a woman or a slave). Democracy was fully developed (unless you were a woman or a slave), lots of building took place, and education was at its zenith (unless you were a woman or a slave—see a pattern here? It's good to be a free man in Ancient Greece).

Every year, Athens held the Panathenaic festivals to honor Athena's birthday, the city's patron goddess. Any Athenian could attend (unless you were a slave. Yay for women!). The festival lasted for days and one of the highlights was the contests—both athletic and musical. If a singer wanted to win a prize (and they all did), he usually recited Homer.

These Athenian singers didn't have the same freedom as their bard counterparts. They couldn't throw lines in willy nilly if they wanted to win the prize. They had to belt out the whole epic in standard form. To help them memorize the "right" version, they first memorized a written poem, just like you do for classes.

It's possible one **tyrant** of Athens had the stories all compiled and written down to help those poor singers out.

> **tyrant:**
> A tyrant wasn't necessarily evil in Ancient Greece—it just meant an aristocratic guy seized power illegally. But he wasn't necessarily a bad ruler. Some were pretty great like Pisistratus who is possibly *the* tyrant who had the Homeric epics written down, and who gave money to farmers to help with their olive crops.

Homer was many things to many people, and that's how he's survived this long. He was better at adapting to the changing times than a cockroach. Who knows, Homer may survive a nuclear apocalypse right along with the roaches. He's already survived thousands of years of war and peace.

Sneakier than a Spy

Homer first impacted his own culture, giving the Greeks heroes with morals they could all aspire to have, including honor, virtue, and fame at all costs. If the Greeks had a Bible, Homer would have been it. Cities like Athens and Sparta would even use passages from the Homeric epics to settle city debates.

Rulers such as Xerxes of Persia and Alexander the Great found all that honor, virtue, and fame pretty heroic. It's no coincidence that both paid their respects to Homer in the Greek way: with sacrifices at Troy, the site of *The Iliad*, before their own major wars.

They say Alexander the Great even slept with a copy of *The Iliad* under his pillow—right next to his knife. Although how he slept with all those long, unwieldy scrolls under his pillow is another question. The idea of a book bound with pages wasn't around yet.

> **excellent in war:**
> This may be his biographer, Arrian, putting words into Alexander's mouth, though.

Alexander claimed *The Iliad* taught him how to be *excellent in war*, and maybe he was onto something. He only consolidated the largest empire the world had ever seen up to that point.

Alexander loved Homer so much that he dreamed of him at night (supposedly). The blind bard would read *The Odyssey* to him and Alexander was all ears. Alexander even had the sneaking suspicion that Homer really wanted him to build a great city in Egypt—the city of Alexandria, to be precise—and all the clues to accomplishing this were in his poems.

All this led to the founding of the Great Library of Alexandria by one of Alexander's generals, which was a pretty big deal. Men (sorry, ladies)

Probably dreaming of the next city to conquer.

sat around discussing the grammar and underlying meanings of these centuries-old stories, among other things. The Great Library of Alexandria also played a part in starting modern Western grammar studies, so really it's Homer you have to thank for weekly grammar quizzes.

The oldest *extant* fragments of Homer's stories come from this time and place—the third century BCE. That doesn't mean the stories weren't written down before then, just that Egypt has great weather for the preservation of papyri scrolls.

extant:
Anything still around today including architectural ruins, papers, and even people.

Next, Homer infiltrated the Roman Empire. He inspired Rome's greatest poet, Virgil, to write his own epic masterpiece, *The Aeneid*, which tells the tale of one survivor from Troy—Aeneas. This epic hero went on to found the Roman people, and Latin, the language the story was written in, went to conquer the world, outlasting even the Romans. (But it's Homer who outlasts everybody.)

While Homer survived the Romans, the Great Library at Alexandria unfortunately did not. Fires ravaged it multiple times over the centuries, and once lost, the scrolls weren't always rewritten. By the seventh century CE, it wasn't around anymore, and lots of **knowledge** vanished forever.

Luckily, by then Homer had fled east to the Byzantine capital—to Constantinople. Despite being a Christian city, Homer escaped the massacre, proving to be as wily as his character, Odysseus. Teachers used Homeric texts as schoolbooks for kids learning to read. Students would copy out thirty to fifty lines of the poems a day, depending on how much of a teacher's pet they wanted to be.

knowledge:

Modern scholars aren't sure how much knowledge was actually lost or even how much there was to begin with, but early sources estimated a ridiculously hard-to-believe range of 34,000 to 700,000 scrolls!

The Byzantine Empire proved the perfect place for Homer to lay low for a thousand years or so. It was stable, and its people spoke Greek. But Homer wasn't done shaping the Western world just yet, and when he finally resurfaced, he did it in his usual style—with a bang.

It's All Greek to Me

By the fifteenth century, no one in Europe could read Homeric Greek anymore, but people still heard about the blind bard. Poet-type people like Geoffrey Chaucer wrote tales about Troy, even though he never read the Homeric stories. In fact, it was the desire to read the actual Homeric stories that got people interested in learning about the Greeks again. Bang.

Okay, so maybe that sounds small fry, but it's not. The new Greek love began an era you might be familiar with already. (Here's a hint: This period involved the likes of Leonardo, Michelangelo, and Raphael, and it's not the Ninja Turtles.)

That's right, you can thank phony Homer for helping to ignite the great rebirth of Western Civilization—the Italian Renaissance. Petrarch and his friend Boccaccio, precursors to the Renaissance, were dying to hear Homer's words. They commissioned the first translation in centuries of *The Iliad* and *The Odyssey*. It wasn't a great translation, but it started something great.

By the middle of the sixteenth century, people could read all about Achilles's rage and Odysseus's cunning once again. (If they could read, that is. The farmer in the dell wasn't reading, and neither were you back then, unless you were important.) That's why there are so many buff, naked Greeks running around Italian paintings and on pages of books. Europeans were obsessed, and it didn't end anytime soon.

With all that renewed interest, people wanted to know if the tales were real. By the nineteenth century, the stories had caught the interest of one Heinrich Schliemann who began a lifelong quest to find historical Troy.

Schliemann's love of all things Homer was awesome, but his methods . . . not so much. He wanted to find Troy, but a few gold coins jingling in his pocket and ancient jewelry for his wife wouldn't hurt either.

In order to find as much gold as possible, he took his spade and dug straight down a huge hill through centuries of cities, destroying the Troy of the *twelfth-century BCE* and a whole bunch of other cities along the way.

The Greek goddess of luck, Tyche, must have been with him though, because the lucky nitwit managed to not only find the gold of Troy, but Mycenae, too, which was the supposed home of Agamemnon.

twelfth-century BCE:

The century when scholars think the Trojan War of The Iliad happened.

His impressive discoveries spurred modern archaeology. Instead of rich noblemen traveling the world and digging up cool, old stuff to show off in their estates, now archeology became more scientific and specialized. The objects found in the ground weren't squirreled away in big houses anymore, but rather catalogued, studied, and put on display in museums for everyone to learn about and enjoy. Of course, we can't give all that credit to Schliemann, since he just took a spade, dug straight down into a hill and struck Troy, but his colleague, Wilhelm Dörpfeld, used his head for more than a hat rack.

During their search for Homer's legendary cities, Dörpfeld noticed something. He realized that the soil had different layers. Eureka! The layers could be used to date all the stuff coming from the soil, just like geologists were already doing for rocks. If a terracotta pot was buried lower than a piece of gold jewelry, then that pot was probably older than the gold. This method has come to be called stratigraphy, and it's the core of archaeology to this day.

Over the years, Homer has helped shaped literature, language, art, and poetry. His legend helped give rise to the Renaissance and to modern archaeology. In many ways, he's the basis for Western civilization. All that, and he didn't even get a Ninja Turtle named after him.

What Do You Think?

Was Homer a poet, a scribe, a compiler, an Alexandrian scholar, an Athenian tyrant, or someone else altogether?

Chapter
10

Prester John

A Real John Doe

Grabbing a Piece of PJ Pie

Prester John was immortal. Until suddenly he wasn't and the world forgot about him. But if this were the year of our Lord, circa 1145, then he would be kind of a big deal. Being immortal and super rich can do that to a guy's reputation.

How big of a deal was Prester John? Well, his kingdom had the Fountain of Youth and rivers that flowed with sparkly jewels instead of boring old water. Europeans—with their decidedly less impressive geography—wanted a piece of the PJ pie, and they didn't care how old and moldy it got. They kept searching for it century after century.

You could say the Europeans were gullible, but that wouldn't do justice to the fact that they undertook two crusades and countless expeditions to Africa and Asia just because of a letter allegedly written by the immortal Prester John himself. Gullible doesn't quite cut it, does it?

Medieval Bishops: More Gossipy than High School Girls?

It all began around 1145, in a setting not too different from a school cafeteria. Bishop Hugh of Jabala went to the court of Pope Eugenius III with an impossible story. A story so crazy the pope couldn't help but believe it. Apparently, Bishop Hugh had heard of a king who also happened to be a priest— and a really powerful one at that. He ruled over vast swaths of land somewhere vaguely in the eastern direction. His holiness was due to his being the great-times-a-lot-grandson of one of the three *Magi*, and his kingliness came from having a lot of soldiers willing to cross a desert.

Magi:

In other words, Prester John was related to one of the three Wise Men who visited the baby Jesus in the New Testament.

According to Bishop Hugh, Prester John recently devastated a group of Muslims called the Samiards. After the most bloody three-day battle you can imagine—yes, worse than Gettysburg—Prester John emerged as the victor. He only had one goal now: march on the holy city of Jerusalem and take the rest of the Islamic world by force. This was exactly the sort of thing medieval popes liked to hear.

The Prester John revelation couldn't have come at a better time, because Bishop Hugh also brought bad news with him. Edessa, an important Christian stronghold, had been captured by Muslim forces. The pope needed an ally, which probably explains why, despite any hard evidence, Eugenius listened to all those dubious rumors and immediately called for the Second *Crusade* to recapture Edessa.

crusades:

A bunch of Holy Wars fought for holy land.

Clearly, having the word "genius" in his name didn't make the pope an Einstein.

He was convinced Prester John would soon be along to help in the fight, even though Bishop Hugh also mentioned how the great Prester John had been stopped from actually getting to Jerusalem by a *river* the first time around.

After defeating the Samiards, Prester John got outwitted by the Tigris. The river was so swollen that Prester John decided to wait for it to freeze over so he and his troops could cross it safely. He waited *years* for the river to ice over, but it never did. (Nobody could accuse John of being a genius, either.) In spite of all that, the pope believed John would be able to cross this time.

The Second Crusade didn't end well for the Christians. As anyone with a frontal lobe could have predicted, Prester John was a no-show. After two years of sieges, the Crusaders still couldn't recapture Edessa, and about the only thing they gained for their trouble was another crusade. Told you it didn't go well.

For the next two decades, the rumors about Prester John stayed just that—rumors. Until 1165, when the most convenient letter in the world showed up. It was from Prester John himself, and it was addressed to Byzantine Emperor Manuel I Comnenus.

Prester John was still around, and he still wanted to stomp on all non-Christians. Addressing Manuel I, he asked the emperor to call him just John. Even though seventy-two (there's that suspicious number again—see chapter 1) kings in the area called him their king, Prester John didn't want to seem mightier than the emperor. Just John would work just fine. And in case anyone thought Prester John wasn't powerful because of that little mishap at the Tigris River, he indulged in some horn-tooting.

This is not going to end well.

The letter declared that he was the richest man in, over, or under the sun, and he had more style than Michael Jordan on or off the court. He had everything from magical plants to magical animals in his kingdom. Even the rocks had healing power. Nobody ever got in fights or was bored, probably because there were too many cool things to explore in his land of milk and honey and jewels. If anyone could number the stars in the sky or count the sands in the sea, then she could also calculate the extent of John's power. It was a challenge nobody but Prester John could win.

The thought of all those riches and healing rocks had European Christians drooling worse than a rabid raccoon. It confirmed everything they thought about the exotic East. It was teeming with gold and all kinds of fantastical things. The lack of a definite location didn't bother them. It just made it easier to imagine Prester John and his wealth anywhere they wanted, and right now they wanted him near Jerusalem.

The letter to the emperor quickly circulated throughout Europe, meaning copies of it got passed around. When the new pope, Alexander III, finally got his copy, he sent his personal physician, Master Philip, to see Prester John. It was the first time a pope sent an envoy to the Far East that didn't include swords and death threats. Instead, he replied along the lines of, "Great, let's get together, but just so you know, you should really stop bragging so much." Popes don't appreciate braggarts.

Philip left in 1177, but which way he went is a mystery. Maybe he knew it was a hopeless quest and took a lifelong vacation instead. Philip was never heard from again.

All of these boasts sound ridiculously made-up, but with about as much worldliness and geographical knowledge as an ant, medieval Europeans couldn't contradict the claims. They really didn't want to, either. They had another crusade to launch, and Prester John was going to help them win it.

He's Just Not into You

Technically speaking, Prester John didn't participate in the Fifth Crusade (1217–1221), but he was there in spirit. Christian Crusaders were told the mighty king already rampaged through the Muslim ranks farther east, and

Christian leaders like Bishop Jacque de Vitry believed Prester John would race to join the slaughter in Egypt when he heard the buzz about the Fifth Crusade.

It's anyone's guess why the Crusaders thought that Prester John would actually show up this time. In an era when news spread about as quick as a snail stuck in glue, it's pretty obvious that he wouldn't make it in time, even if the letter wasn't a fake (it was) and the great king existed (he didn't).

But the Europeans really wanted to beat the snot out of the Muslims, and they were willing to entertain all kinds of delusions to keep their hope alive. Prester John was more than delusional propaganda—he was hope that Christians were out there in the East. He was that ratty, old security blanket we all used to carry around, except it would take centuries to let this one go.

Besides, in 1219, Europeans believed that monsters and unicorns lived behind the shrubs in their backyards, which really puts things in perspective. An immortal king doesn't seem that strange. So, full of hope, the Europeans set off to yet another war.

Predictably, the Fifth Crusade went much like the Second, which is to say poorly. Prester John never showed his immortal face. No word on what held him up this time.

After Prester John jilted them once again, you'd think the Europeans would've gotten the hint. He just wasn't into them. Or maybe they would've zeroed in on the real reason—Prester John was a bonafide fake and the letter a very creative forgery—but they *didn't*.

didn't:
Even centuries later, in 1400, people were still asking Prester John to join the fight. Henry IV of England wrote him a note asking to crusade with him, like he might finally show up or something. They were always hopeful, if not always smart. Not surprisingly, Henry IV died before he got a reply from the famous priest-king.

Look Alive!

After the Fifth Crusade, hope rose again from the ashes, just like the phoenix Prester John claimed to have. It wouldn't last long, though. Bishop Jacques de Vitry now heard that there was a ruler on the Asian plains who had mobilized against the Muslim infidels.

Foiled again! It's just Genghis Khan.

Yes! This sounded a lot like Prester John's M.O. The Europeans got extremely excited, and when Europeans got excited, invasions usually weren't far off.

This time, though, they were the ones getting invaded. "Prester John" turned out to be just Genghis Khan trying his hand at world domination. When the Mongols started conquering European lands in 1237, no one believed the khan was Prester John anymore, despite their rhyming names. Maybe it was time to stop listening to gossipy bishops.

Marco Polo, known to travel a lot, tried to clear up all the confusion. He had lived with the Mongols since he was a teenager and according to him, there had been a priest who was also a king, and probably the one Europeans called Prester John (score!), but Genghis Khan had defeated and killed him already (boo!).

You'd think Marco Polo would have had some influence over the European Christians in terms of clearing up the mystery of Prester John, being that Polo was a famous travel writer and all, but apparently not. His account didn't stop future writers in the thirteenth and fourteenth centuries from keeping the search for the infamous priest-king alive. Some legends die hard—especially alluring ones about immortality and riches.

Thanks to another man who never existed, the legend of Prester John continued to grow and spread. Sir John Mandeville—or at least someone using that pen name—wrote a travel book in the mid-fourteenth century gushing about Prester John's imaginary kingdom filled with unbelievable sights. Horned cannibals lived there in peace with strange humans who cried instead of talked. Sir John also claimed that the kingdom had more gems

travel:

Mandeville's travels were what you call armchair travels. He made it all up from his nice cozy armchair, and stole from others when he got writer's block.

and jewels than King Midas. According to Mandeville, even Prester John's bed was made of gold and sapphires and had magical properties.

Mandeville's *"travel"* narrative sold pretty well, probably because the mystery author had more creativity than J. K. Rowling with all those creatures he made up.

The book was translated into many different languages and was considered one of the most popular non-religious books published during the medieval period. Thanks to Mandeville's imagination, many explorers to the New World combed the land in search of hybrid humans, Prester John, and the Fountain of Youth.

Breaking News!

If a news article came out today boasting about finding a magical land filled with headless cannibals, birds on fire, and the secret to immortality, we can safely assume that only a few people would be gullible enough to believe it. Even fewer would sell all their possessions and go searching for the place in question. But that's not how life (and people) worked during the medieval era. Despite the lack of fantastical creatures roaming the European countryside, people didn't doubt that they existed. Their prayer books, called psalters, were filled with beautiful illustrations, and while most illuminated run-of-the-mill, daily-life activities, an odd creature always found its way onto the margins.

While the medieval mind was a fertile ground for creatures, the people of that era gained a lot of their ideas about the world from ancient writers. In their minds, if it was old, then it was gold. That means that if Pliny the Elder, famous Roman writer and military commander, said there were one-eyed people and fiery birds living on the edges of the known world (Africa or Asia), then there probably were.

Thanks to them, interest in monsters lasted and tons of bestiaries were produced. In tenth-century England, someone compiled a book called *Wonders of the East*, and it had loads of pictures of men with their heads in their chests. It makes you wonder: Did Prester John's author take a peek at this book, or Pliny's pages, before penning those letters?

On the Map

All that chatter was enough to start putting Prester John on the map. Mapmakers weren't sure where he lived—only that he ruled over the Three Indies. Back then, the Three Indies could be anything to the south or east of Jerusalem, which is kind of a big area. It could include what we today call Africa, Asia, and the Americas.

Obviously, medieval Europeans didn't have the first clue about geography, but the search for Prester John gave them the opportunity to learn. Prester John's fingerprints are all over—either directly or indirectly—every exploration into Asia and Africa during the medieval period and even into the modern era.

The first maps with Prester John's kingdom noted on them appeared in 1320. Then, for the next couple centuries, mapmakers switched gears and

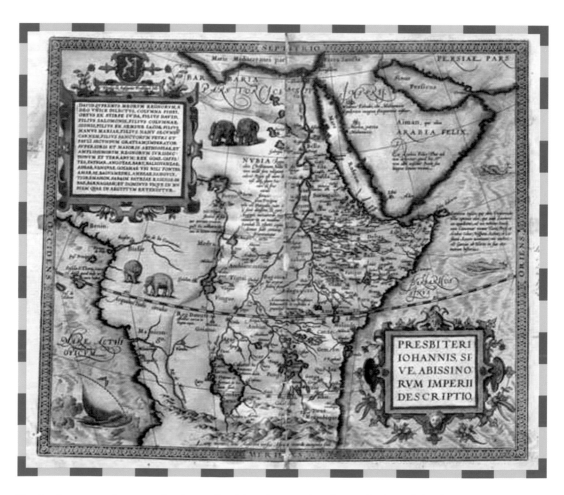

Maybe the mapmaker was sipping on lead-laced wine when he made this oddly shaped African map.

threw him and his kingdom in Africa, with a few rogue maps clinging to Asia. An atlas from 1606 gives Prester John a full-page spread and in a big-hearted gesture, granted 30 percent of Africa to the fake king.

In 1477, *Geographia*, a book by the famous ancient geographer Ptolemy, found its way to Europe. It had strange references to a place that sounded—if you crossed your eyes and squinted really hard—a lot like Prester John's kingdom. Hallelujah! Confirmation, at last. Obviously, if a smart man like Ptolemy referenced Prester John's kingdom centuries ago, it must have truly existed.

Just in case anybody still had doubts, two more letters surfaced from Prester John in 1500—one addressed to the emperor of Rome and the other to the king of France. It didn't bother anybody that over three hundred years had passed since the first letter. After all, Prester John was immortal. Thanks to the newly invented printing press, the 1500 equivalent of going viral meant over one hundred copies of the bestselling letter circulated throughout Europe.

With new details about his kingdom, Prester John had Europe in a tizzy again. (Of course, more invasions weren't far off, but Europeans now called them "explorations.") The new letters painted a vivid picture and it was weird indeed. It described the exotic animals and bizarre humans in Prester John's faraway land. In fact, Prester John's kingdom now sounded suspiciously populated with Mandeville's creations: men with their heads in their chests, Amazonian women, griffins, and phoenixes. Its Fountain of Youth could even turn bathers back to the stylish age of thirty-two.

All of these claims seem fantastical to us, but they weren't so crazy at the time. The world was a big, scary place in the sixteenth century, and remember—monsters and unicorns were everywhere. There might be dragons in the Indies, but there might also be Prester John, at least according to some *early explorers*.

It might have been a stretch, but the Europeans stretched so far, they were practically silly

early explorers:

Jordan Catalani traveling in 1324 to India reported that both dragons and Prester John were probably in the Horn of Africa, which was considered part of the "Indies" at the time. He was the first to scoot the priest-king to Africa. Now, of course, everyone wanted the phony king in that vicinity.

A face only a mother can love.

putty, and totally fine with that. That was especially true of the Portuguese, who started thinking to themselves, *Man, we really have to find this guy.*

Fool Me Once . . .

The Portuguese were Prester John "superfans." They never gave up believing in his far-off kingdom. Because the Portuguese were constantly fighting with their Muslim neighbors, called the Moors, the idea of an invincible Christian ally looked as tantalizing as filling up on dessert before a dinner of brussel sprouts.

Because it turned out that Genghis Khan wasn't Prester John, and because it would be really convenient for them, the Portuguese took to the idea of

John in Africa like a hermit crab to a shell. Secretly, they sent ambassadors to find the famed king, and no one was more determined to discover the elusive kingdom than Prince Henry the Navigator.

Don't be fooled by his name. While Prince Henry the Navigator did create an institute for astronomy, navigation, shipbuilding, and research, he never actually went on any of his own expeditions. Why risk his own life when he could pay other people to do it? In fact, he rarely left his home in Portugal, but that didn't stop him from being obsessed with Prester John. He instructed all of his ship captains to not only tap into the goody bag of Africa (i.e., gold, ivory, and slaves), but to also search out their Christian ally, Prester John.

Even the current pope was taken in by the possibility of an alliance with Prester John. Pope Nicolas V issued a papal bull in 1455 calling on all Europeans to help Prince Henry in his quest to find Prester John. Then, Prince Henry died, and it was up to his nephew, King John II of Portugal, to find the mythical king.

King John II is known for a lot of things, like making Portugal powerful and sending out explorers to new lands practically every other day. Sadly, finding Prester John isn't one of those things. His explorers did discover the Congo River, round the Cape of Good Hope, and travel to India, but they didn't find the elusive priest-king. Instead, his explorers found morbidly hairy, yet extremely tiny humans living in trees in the heart of Africa.

That stoked their imaginations. If men could come in pint-sized, seriously hairy packages, maybe one-eyed men and birds on fire were somewhere out there too. (What they'd really found were monkeys, in case you were curious.)

So Close, Yet, So Far

Deep into the fifteenth century, Europe was still hopeful about their odds of finding Prester John. They'd be poor gamblers, though. In 1492, a guy named Christopher Columbus decided to go all in.

He dreamed of getting to the East by sailing west and maybe finding some Prester John wonders along the way. He didn't let little things get in the way of his dreams, like "no's" from multiple monarchs or the facts. He relied on whatever sounded coolest to decide his trip, including legends and rumors.

Columbus even admitted, "For the execution of the voyage to the Indies, I did not make use of intelligence, mathematics, or maps."

But he did use books. (Although, they were really more like novels, which would be like using *The Hunger Games* as a survival guide.) Columbus's library was full of ancient "histories" by Pliny and Plutarch that mixed fact and fiction in blender-like fashion.

Columbus doesn't reference the Prester John legend directly in any of his letters or diaries, but he does frequently mention the works of Sir John Mandeville and Marco Polo. He even wrote sprawling notes in the margins next to their fantastical stories and used their travels as his guidebook. It's no wonder Columbus had crazy ideas regarding what he might find when he blindly groped his way toward the New World.

When he finally got his "yes" from the king and queen of Spain to set sail for the Indies, his imagination kept him going. It also allowed him to believe manatees were mermaids and that he'd reached the Spice Islands of India, even though there were no spices, only confused natives in what were

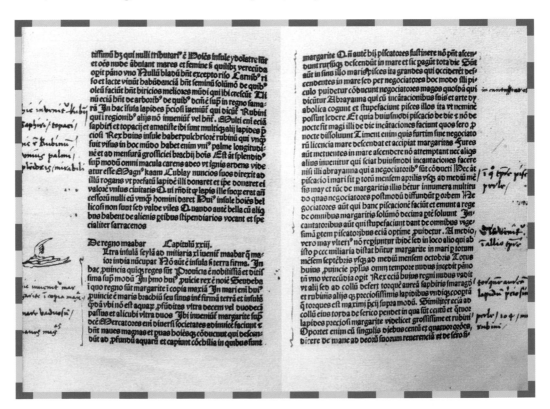

Take a page out of Columbus's book; just don't expect to find India.

I'm telling you, man. There's something off about these girls . . .

actually the islands of the Caribbean. He probably hoped to find Prester John among the natives and take a dip or two in the Fountain of Youth.

Instead of finding the mythical king, he gets credit for finding North America, even if he wasn't the first, and even if he never set boot there.

End of an Era

You have to admire the Europeans' resiliency. Even into the seventeenth century, there was no shortage of travelers searching for Prester John. It wasn't until a German scholar named Hiob Ludolf turned his attention to Prester John that the legend finally started to fade.

Ludolf proved there was no connection between the great king and the legends swirling around him, and the world soon forgot him entirely. The Age

Will the Real Prester John Please Stand Up?

So Prester John was a big fake, and sadly, there was never a real person who came close to being like him. But there were a few individuals who provided just the right touch of inspiration to spark five hundred years of speculation, crusades, and European exploration. Here are a couple of them:

Yelü Dashi

In 1141, Yelü Dashi defeated the Seljuk Turks, and although he wasn't a priest or a Christian, he *was* an Eastern king winning battles against Muslims. Bishop Hugh may have taken real events, muddled them accidently (or not so accidently), and created Prester John out of the stories of this Eastern warrior king.

Ethiopian Emperors

After "dying" in Mongolia at the hands of Genghis Khan, the Prester John legend hopped over to Ethiopia. One European explorer, Pêro da Covilhã, thought he had even found the great priest-king, but it turned out to be Emperor Eskender of the Ethiopians instead. That didn't stop the Europeans from calling the Ethiopian emperors by the honorific title of Prester John for centuries after—much to the surprise of the Ethiopian emperors.

of Exploration was over and with it, the Age of Prester John. He finally fell off the map. Literally. The last map to include Prester John's kingdom dates to the late-seventeenth century.

Although the fake king never existed, he left his calling card all over history. His legend launched crusades and inspired Europeans during the Middle Ages to explore their world and expand their knowledge beyond their borders. Along the way, crusaders and explorers plundered lands and killed or enslaved countless numbers of innocent people, but it's hard to hold a fake guy accountable for the greedy actions of those who really lived and breathed.

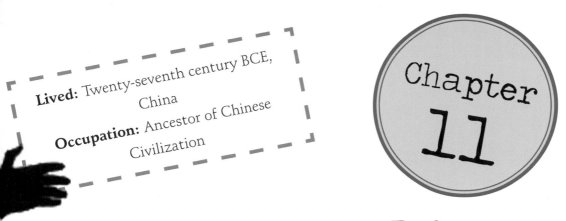

Lived: Twenty-seventh century BCE, China

Occupation: Ancestor of Chinese Civilization

Chapter 11

Huangdi

The Yellow Emperor Strikes Back

The Yellow Emperor Strikes Back

What emperor chased a rebel, didn't mind a little violence, and called up a magical force to help control an army? If you said the galactic Emperor from *Star Wars*, you'd be close, but you'd be wrong.

Huangdi (pronounced Hwahng-dee), the Yellow Emperor of mythical China, may not have chased Luke Skywalker around the galaxy, but his influence echoed across time and space, just like the evil Emperor Palpatine. They even had similar tactics, like using organized violence to maintain discipline in their empires. Okay, sure, instead of building the Death Star, Huangdi rode into battle on horseback and unified the rebels. And instead of using the Force, the Yellow Emperor called upon the drought goddess, Ba, for help. Besides that, they're practically the same.

Including the fact that neither of them existed, those phonies.

Usually, a legend grows around a real person whose memory blows up to epic proportions. Not so with the Yellow Emperor. In fact, it's kind of the opposite. Huangdi started out as the sky god, Shangdi (pronounced Shang-dee), which seems like a better gig. Eventually, he morphed into a man, who then became a god again. Confused? Don't worry, so is everybody else.

My other ride is a yellow dragon.

Supposedly, the Yellow Emperor ruled around the twenty-seventh century BCE, and while it's hard enough to verify the lives of people that far back in history, it becomes oh-so-complicated when the first records of his name come 2,300 years later.

From God to Man and Back Again

One of the early Chinese gods, Shangdi, figured into a lot of myths over the course of Chinese civilization. Even the earliest dynasties knew about Shangdi. His name looks a lot like Huangdi's in Chinese. Some think that those living in the Warring States Period remembered the old stories, reworked them, and created a legendary emperor who represented their times, making everybody scratch their heads.

Huangdi is from the probably mythical dynasty that includes the likes of fellow sage emperors Yao and Yu the Engineer. While Huangdi didn't get as cool a nickname as Yu, he became the supreme ruler of the five sages from this legendary period (a.k.a., the good ol' days).

Even if the job didn't technically exist, the Yellow Emperor definitely got better publicity than the Galactic Emperor. He's sailed through history as the ancestor of everything Chinese, all thanks to some guys during a time called the Warring States Period, which, as you might imagine, waged a lot of wars.

Gentlemen Don't Start Fights . . .

The Yellow Emperor's legend starts with your typical half-dragon, half-human baby story. He rose to power in the regular fashion—that is, by brute force. He lived on the plains of Guanzhong (pronounced Guan-sha-ow), but instead of hunting and foraging like everyone else, he preferred kicking butt and taking names. Seriously. After he defeated one tribe and brought them into his fold, he'd take that tribe's name into his own.

First on his list was the Yan Emperor, head of a plains tribe. Some of the other tribe leaders didn't like the way Yan was looking at them; it kind of seemed like he wanted them. So they asked Huangdi for help. Huangdi saw rampant disorder all over and knew there was only one thing he could do. Huangdi decided it was time to take control of Yan's men for Yan's own good. You snooze, you lose, Yan.

As you can imagine, Yan didn't quite agree with this assessment so the only thing left to do was to duke it out in the first big battle of Chinese history: the Battle of Banquan. (Note: extremely legendary. Possibly never happened. Evidence scarce.)

Luckily for Huangdi, he just so happened to have tamed six wild beasts before the battle, including bears and tigers. They really helped turn the tide in Huangdi's favor. The Yan Emperor realized he was no match for these beasts and formed an alliance. Huangdi named the new, larger tribe Yan Huang, and they planned to have a swell time ruling the plains together.

Of course, people were jealous of Huangdi's new tribe and all his power, even though he was only trying to keep the peace through war. Nothing wrong with that. However, Chi You (pronounced Chih-Yo) decided he was the rebel to challenge Huangdi. Some say he was a jealous minister to Huangdi; others say that he was a random guy on the plains who would have really enjoyed WWE or UFC (if such things had been around). If Chi You had been able to take his aggression out in a cage match, maybe he wouldn't have tried to take it out on Huangdi.

Either way, Chi You led over seventy tribes against Huangdi in an all-or-nothing smackdown. It didn't go Huangdi's way this time. He may have tamed multiple beasts, but Chi You's soldiers were made of bronze, which sounds suspiciously like men wearing suits of armor. Except bronze smelting hadn't been discovered yet, and the oldest bronze armor ever discovered dates from 1,500 years after this battle.

After Huangdi's humiliating defeat, he went up into the mountains to have a long think about what went wrong against the vicious Chi You. Like a three-year think.

While there, a goddess came to help him as they tend to do for heroes. She gave him sacred texts and tools that would turn the battle from a merely physical confrontation into a mental art. No more running around like mad, screaming and waving a sword. Huangdi would have to have style on the battlefield.

The next time Chi You and Huangdi met was at The Battle of Zhoulu, which would decide the fate of all the tribes living on the plains. The fight didn't start the way Huangdi hoped. For one, Chi You started burping out fog that made it hard to see, but Huangdi had a solution for that. He invented the South-Pointing Chariot, which is a chariot that points south, to help his soldiers out of the fog.

Chi You --in serious need of a cage match

Then, Chi You made it rain. Instead of cats and dogs, it was more like demons and chaos and more rain. Huangdi called on his goddess friend, Ba, to conjure up a drought and dry out the land. It's possible that Ba was also his daughter, which would make it easier to ask for help. Having solved the rain and fog issue, Huangdi captured Chi You. Since Huangdi didn't want any demon blood on his hands, a dragon came down and slew the rebel for him.

All the tribes around the Yellow River were now his. Next on his list: world domination! Just kidding. Being the ancestor of all Han Chinese was good enough for Huangdi.

But They Finish Them

After all that war, the plains got a lot of peace, which led to a golden age. Before Huangdi, people wandered from tree to tree searching for safe places to sleep each night. As cool as a tree house sounds, it wasn't as nice as a fluffy bed. He also showed them how to cook their food and tame animals, like he did for the battle. In other words, he created civilization, because without these things, humans were one small step away from being beasts themselves.

Huangdi didn't stop there. Besides the South-Pointing Chariot, which was both a compass and a chariot, he created other vehicles like boats and carts, bowls for all that newly cooked food, a calendar, and *cuju*, a form of Chinese soccer. Huangdi wasn't selfish. He let his loyal ministers get in on the action, too. His historian invented the Chinese character system in order to better record Huangdi's awesomeness. His minister invented bamboo flutes and found the five tones and twelve scales needed to bring beautiful music to Huangdi's ears.

Even Huangdi's wives seemed to have a special touch. One invented chopsticks to go along with the bowls, and another came up with an idea for a comb. As cool as chopsticks and combs are, Huangdi's most famous wife, Lei Zu, discovered something even better—a worm that burped up pure perfection! Okay, not perfection, but close enough. She discovered

Huangdi's brilliance in a nutshell.

the secret to raising silkworms after a cocoon dropped in her afternoon cup of *tea*. The worms weren't exactly burping up silk, but spitting it up to make their cocoons. The heat of the tea unwound the silk of the cocoon, which is actually silkworm spit.

After Lei Zu figured out the threads were soft as well as strong, she invented the silk loom and taught people how to make luxurious clothes fit for an empress, which happened to be her. Legend says she was the ugliest woman around, but Huangdi liked her best since she was smart.

tea:

Although tea drinking wasn't a national custom until the eighth century CE during the Tang dynasty. Details!

In reality, most of these things weren't invented until centuries later during (and even after) China's Bronze Age, but that didn't stop people from tacking their inventions onto the legend of the most famous sage, the Yellow Emperor.

Despite Huangdi being the personification of perfection, he couldn't stay on earth ruling forever. A yellow dragon eventually came calling and whisked him away to heaven, making Huangdi immortal. No word on whether the dragon was related to him.

For the next two thousand years, give or take a few centuries, things got pretty quiet for Huangdi.

Classics of Internal Medicine

This first book of medicine in Chinese history had a lot of radical ideas rolling around its pages. It included pearls of wisdom like demons *not* causing illness. At a time when Western doctors still believed a woman became sick when her womb went wandering, this was pretty on track.

Even though *Classics of Internal Medicine* was written during the Warring States Period (two thousand years after Huangdi "lived"), the text is supposedly a conversation between Huangdi and his ministers in the form of questions and answers. To them, old age, lack of exercise, bad diets, and rowdy emotions caused sickness. Sure, the diagnosis could be off the wall sometimes and often depended on things like the time of day, the season, and the gender of the patient, but the treatments were better than the hang-upside-down-for-a-day solutions the Greeks had in rotation around the same time. And the holistic knowledge imparted in the text is still used today in Eastern (and some Western) treatments, like acupuncture, circadian rhythms, and ying and yang.

You Can't Stop Violence without More Violence

The Warring States Period didn't get its name by handing out flowers and candy every day. Instead, nobles handed out dagger-axes and swords and generally made life hard for regular people. If they had a motto it would have been: only violence stops violence.

It was a chaotic time and the Warring States elite looked to old stories, legends, and myths to help them stake a claim to someone else's land. They justified a whole bunch of stuff based on these stories, as well as the new

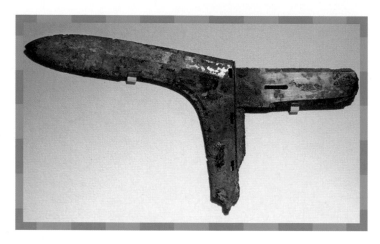

Nothing says, "Welcome to the neighborhood" like a dagger-axe.

A Pit Stop on the Way to Immortality

On his dragon-mounted trip to immortality, Huangdi decided to take a brief detour. In order to comfort his people, he dismounted in Yan'an City to say goodbye and to plant a cypress tree. This was a bad idea. His people didn't want to be comforted. They wanted Huangdi to stay. As he tried to slip away on his dragon, they tore off his clothes and Huangdi had to flee butt naked.

Today, Huangdi's mausoleum (a really big tomb) is located on the site, and yearly offerings have been made to his honor on and off since the Warring States Period. The cypress tree survives as well as an imprint of Huangdi's feet.

Huangdi had a light step.

ones they made up about the sage emperors.

Since Huangdi pretty much lived the dream life— one guy conquering all the other guys—it's no surprise that the Warring States nobles pegged him as their hero. His name appears for the first time in writing during this period (despite the fact that Huangdi invented writing). A bronze vessel mentions his name and the convenient fact that the Yellow Emperor had just used ***Tian*** to overthrow his enemies. People liked the sound of that.

He's mentioned in passing in other texts, too, mostly associated with the idea of ruling by force. One text really liked the idea of killing as punishment and claimed the

Tian:

Heaven.

modern state came from Huangdi. The strong should overcome the weak and tell them what to do, just like Huangdi, otherwise everyone would go back to being beasts again. After all, Huangdi was made immortal, so it must be okay. Right‽

In the end, all of these stories about Huangdi tell us one thing, and it wasn't a biography of his fabulous life. They tell us what the Warring States elite thought and honored above all else. War, duh.

A Period of War and Thoughtfulness?

Interestingly, the chaotic Spring and Autumn Period and the Warring States Period are also the time of the Hundred Schools of Thought. Since there wasn't one guy running around with a tiara on his head making up all the rules, lots of people had lots of ideas about the best way to live and govern. In addition to the ideas attributed to Huangdi, this time period boasts such legends as Confucius and Sun Tzu, author of The Art of War. Legalism and Daoism were also created during this time period, and Huangdi is connected to both.

After all those years of fighting, the last man standing was Qin Shi Huangdi (pronounced Chin Shee Hwahng-dee), the first emperor of the first dynasty, the Qin (say: Chin) Dynasty (221–206 BCE). Of course it's no coincidence that he had a similar name to the Yellow Emperor. Qin Shi meant to do that. It gave him more power and prestige as a ruler. It must have worked, too, since Qin Shi began the tradition of Chinese emperors that didn't end until 1911. He also passed on the tradition of adding "Huangdi" to each new emperor's name.

Qin Shi, like his namesake, enjoyed the idea of ruling by force. Things didn't exactly pan out for Joe Schmos during this time. They got conned into things like building the beginnings of the **Great Wall**. This really did suck, with 300,000 people dying to build those original foundations. But he also unified China after the Warring States Period, standardized writing and weights, and started a national road system.

Great Wall:

Eventually, the Great Wall got its other, less flattering, nickname: the longest cemetery on earth. It's estimated a million people died during construction. But that's just an estimate.

Qin Shi liked one more thing about his man, Huangdi. He really liked the way Huangdi never died.

Don't Count Your Dragon Eggs Till They Hatch

Jumping on the back of a dragon and flying to heaven to become immortal sounded like the perfect ending to Qin Shi's own story. At least, Qin Shi was sold. This immortality thing really suited an emperor. Qin Shi wasn't one to sit around and just dream, so he sent out searchers to find the secret to immortality ASAP.

He didn't put all his dragon eggs in one basket. Qin Shi prepped for the worst by having an entire force of terracotta warriors assembled over the course of thirty-seven years specially gift wrapped for his own tomb. The clay warriors' mission was to protect him and to help him rule over another empire; one in the afterlife.

Qin Shi's terracotta soldier—probably to protect the Emperor in the next life from all the people who died building his Great Wall.

To make them more realistic, every warrior was unique. There are over eight thousand warriors in Qin Shi's tomb, not including chariots, horses, acrobats, musicians, and officials. All for Qin Shi's pleasure. He was definitely ready, just in case his people never found the secret to immortality. And according to our records, they didn't.

Even though he finally realized he wouldn't find personal immortality in this world, Qin Shi thought his dynasty would last forever. It hung on for three more years after he died, officially the shortest dynasty in Chinese history. According to the next rulers, the Hans, Qin Shi was a brutal, book-burning ruler who lost the Mandate of Heaven (see chapter 1), and they weren't exactly wrong.

While Qin Shi may have begun the tradition of Chinese emperors, it was the Hans that decided just about *everything else* until 1911.

Luckily for Huangdi, the Han emperor, Wudi (pronounced Woo-dee), installed Confucian principles as the main guidelines for life. He included rulers acting like the sage emperors in order to get their own shot at immortality—in other words, acting like Huangdi. Unluckily for everyone else, Wudi ended up not being so different from Qin Shi after all. By the last few decades of his fifty-four-year reign, only one of his seven chancellors died a natural death.

Besides getting his kicks off of chopping up everyone from commoners to family members, Wudi also enjoyed the idea of immortality of the Huangdi variety.

Like Qin Shi, Wudi could totally see himself flying around on a dragon of his very own all the way up to heaven with all his ladies, feeling the wind in his hair and eating dewdrops. But the ladies weren't necessary. He (supposedly)

everything else:

Including the Confucian craze, the spread of Buddhism, the Silk Road, and inventions like paper, porcelain, and a seismograph for detecting earthquakes. The Han wrote the first history book of China and started China's love of jade for its mystical properties. They were regarded as the most powerful dynasty in Chinese history, and other dynasties liked to reminisce and look to them for inspiration on how to unite an empire. The ethnic Chinese still refer to themselves as the Han.

A naked man ran by here.

said, "If I could become like the Yellow Emperor, I would leave my wife and children behind without hesitation." Considering he went through women pretty quickly, this isn't hard to imagine.

To keep all the good mojo flowing Huangdi's way, and to give himself a great chance at immortality, Wudi and the rest of the Han continued to make sacrifices to the Yellow Emperor and built another shrine at the mausoleum at Yan'an. Today, the mausoleum is a symbol of the Chinese nation and remains important in the current politics of the country, even getting special festivities every April.

How to Survive the Centuries

As you may have noticed, the twentieth century is when everything changed for China. Emperors were no longer around, and the country went bananas. Again.

In 1911, the Qing (pronounced Ching) emperors were overthrown and the Republic of China was born.

The buzzword became *Zhonghua Minzu*.

To them, Zhonghua Minzu consisted of the Han and four other ethnic groups, which made up one big, happy family. It was like the Brady Bunch on a dragon-sized scale, but they called it the Five Races Under One Union. It's probably easy to guess who the father was. Huangdi was still around, and now he wasn't just the father of the Han, but of all five groups. Times looked good for Huangdi.

Zhonghua Minzu:

A nickname for one big Chinese family.

That is, until two more revolutions arose, including the Cultural Revolution in the 1960s. The man in charge, Mao Zedong, didn't appreciate tradition or all those ancestors. Too many cobwebs. Anything that was considered old or ancient was smashed. This included everything from old artifacts to old culture to old people.

As the ancestor of ancestors, Huangdi pretty much epitomized old stuff, so for a decade (1966 1976) he slunk around in hiding. But Huangdi had

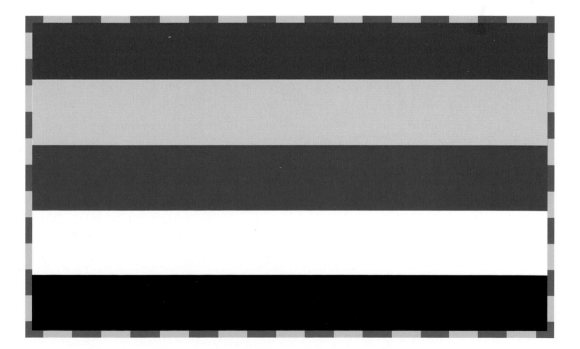

Five Races Under One Union

already survived thousands of years. He could wait a mere ten more to steal the spotlight again.

By the 1980s, Mao was dead and Huangdi was back, and he had an even bigger role. Now Huangdi wasn't just the ancestor of the five ethnic groups, but of fifty-six.

That's a lot of kids for Huangdi to support.

It hasn't always been one big happy family, though. The claim that all fifty-six groups descended from Huangdi has been used to rationalize China's expansion in the region. Huangdi is probably used to all the politics, but instead of justifying invasions in the Warring States Period, he's justifying invasions in the modern period. Which is pretty convenient for Huangdi.

More Political Than Human

Whether he was only an oral tradition, a god, or just an invention of sly storytelling elitists, in the end, Huangdi was never an actual man. Almost five thousand years later this legend is still being used in political maneuvers in China.

Just remember, stories of the Yellow Emperor were first recorded over two *thousand* years after he supposedly took to the sky on his dragon. If this story doesn't smell as questionable as rotting fish hanging out in a barrel under direct sunlight for a week, then your nose must be broken.

In the end, it's important to remember that stories reflect the times in which they were written—not the actual times they describe. Including the new ones. End of story.

Chapter 12

Lived: Eighteenth to nineteenth century CE, Europe, America

Occupation: Chess-playing Automaton

The Turk

Practically the Terminator

A Whopper of a Lie

Automata were the dinosaurs of computers.

They didn't chomp on ferns (or other dinosaurs, if they were the carnivorous kind). Rather, they were an ancient type of robot. Some were even programmable—like a computer. Instead of doing complicated logarithms or downloading the latest app, they did the same thing over and over again.

Many told the time—you can call them clocks. Some were human-like and moved their arms or heads up and down, ensuring nightmares for life for little kids. Some were used to amuse, like the mechanical duck that "digested" food and pooped it out. But maybe the greatest thing an automaton ever did was help inspire two revolutions—the Industrial and the computer.

automata:

More than one robot.

Whatever you do, don't imagine her coming to life at night.

Well, sort of.

The Turk, a chess-playing **automaton** in the eighteenth and nineteenth centuries, was arguably the most famous automaton of all time. He traveled the world, fascinating kings, queens, scientists, and inventors. He was the inspiration behind some of the most important inventions in the history of human kind.

automaton:
One robot.

Only problem, he was a total fake. See if you can figure out the hoax of the Turk.

Anything You Can Do, I Can Do Better

Eighteenth-century European elites were used to being wooed. They had everyone kissing their aristocratic behinds, including all kinds of riff-raff who wanted their patronage (i.e., their money). So in order to impress them, inventors had to be impressive.

Wolfgang von Kempelen, inventor extraordinaire, never wanted to build the chess-player. He just wanted to be a scientist, but he picked a really bad time to stick his foot in his mouth. He did it in front of his queen.

During a performance by a French conjurer, Wolfgang leaned into Maria Theresa, Queen of Hungary and Bohemia, and Archduchess of Austria (not to mention Holy Roman Empress), and dismissively explained what he thought was going on—a loud show of noise, smoke, and mirrors with a few automata doing tricks his dog could do in his sleep. Kempelen claimed that he could do better. So the Queen told him to prove it. Kempelen's mouth probably dropped to the floor, which would've made it easier to get his foot out.

She excused him from his court duties and told him to crack at it. She also told him he better not fail: this was a matter of national pride. So Kempelen spent the next six months building his deceptive masterpiece.

red herrings:
Not actual fish, but distractions or fake outs to hide what's really going on.

Throwing Red Fish

Every great magician knows that it's imperative to throw a couple of **red herrings** at the audience to misdirect them. Luckily for Kempelen, he was a master performer. When he finally unveiled his automaton, he had the queen and everybody else at court eating out of the palm of his hand.

He told them that the Turk was more than a mere clockwork, wind-up automaton—he was an intelligent, fast-thinking, chess-playing marvel that could beat the pants off anyone in Europe.

First, Kempelen brought out his life-size automaton, which was a mechanical man who sat behind a huge wooden box looking very exotic and smoking a pipe (smoking was the cool kid thing to do in late eighteenth-century Europe). The automaton had dark skin and wore a turban and a tunic with bright billowing sleeves (during that time, exotic servants were also cool).

Kempelen announced to an intrigued audience that he had created an automaton that could play chess. That's right! It didn't need pre-determined moves like all the other automata out there. It could think for itself. (It was one step away from turning into the Terminator.)

In order to prove to his skeptical audience that there weren't any children chess masters secretly hiding inside, Kempelen opened the box and stuck a candle inside. The audience saw some complicated machinery and the back wall. Positive that everyone believed it was empty except for clockwork, he then set up a chess-board, wound up the Turk, and asked for a victim . . . um . . . volunteer.

The Turk made the first move. He could pick up any piece and make any move, but that wasn't all. If a player tried cheating, the Turk called him out on it. He'd pick up the offending move, put it back, and went ahead with his own turn, shaking his head sadly at the cheater. If the player tried cheating again, the Turk would clear the board with a sweep of his hand. After all, even robots have morals.

The Turk usually beat his opponent within half an hour. He

Even robots have feelings.

took no prisoners. Not one to dally, he quickly blew through the Austrian court. The astonished queen insisted that Kempelen trot out the Turk whenever an important visitor came to Vienna to show off this amazing invention. She was bursting with national pride now.

You'd think Kempelen would have been thrilled. He had impressed the queen and fulfilled his promise. But he wasn't happy at all. Devastated might describe it better. He wanted to be a scientist, not an inventor for the court's entertainment. For a while, he tried pretending that the Turk was broken, but it didn't work for long. Maria Theresa always seemed to see right through his bluffs. Finally, Queen Maria Theresa died and Kempelen dismantled the Turk—for good, he thought.

He was wrong.

Around Europe in Two Years

Soon after taking the throne, the new king, Joseph II, insisted that Kempelen bring the Turk out of retirement when Russian royalty came to court. This was exactly the sort of thing Kempelen didn't want to be suckered into doing again, but you don't say no to a king. Not if you enjoy keeping all your body parts.

Maybe Kempelen should have sabotaged the Turk during that performance, because it did such a good job of pummeling everyone into submission that King Joseph II insisted he show it off to the rest of Europe. A two-year vacation touring Europe doesn't sound like the worst thing in the world to most people, but Kempelen wasn't most people. He wanted to be taken seriously as a scientist, but when a king made a request, he knew to break out his passport.

playing:

This was considered an acceptable way to spend your time back when a person could make a living playing chess blindfolded.

Paris was a chess-playing hot spot, so Kempelen took his act there first. Chess masters sat around all day *playing* in cafes, so a giant automaton with a built-in table fit right in.

The Turk was a roaring success in the City of Lights. During Kempelen's Parisian visit, many tried to discover the secret of the Turk, but they all failed. Kempelen was too crafty for those Frenchmen.

He never touched the Turk, except to wind him up every once in a while or to tap his fingers on the box as a distraction. Sometimes, just to prove how self-sufficient the Turk was, Kempelen hung out in the audience while the robot beat chess greats from all over the continent like a drum. Victorian Europe was baffled and bewitched. The Turk didn't always win, but he won enough to make people suspicious of it and of Kempelen.

Theories about the Turk ranged from the absurd to the more absurd. It didn't help when a chess-playing monkey turned up in Baghdad. One theory claimed that Kempelen had hired the monkey and slipped him inside the Turk's sleeves with a few bananas to keep his chess master happy. (No monkeys were hurt—or even involved— in the making of this show.)

Some people insisted Kempelen used black magic to beat the chess players. Another popular theory was that little people were hidden inside the Turk. Others stuck to the more scientific line of reasoning, such as the use of magnets and machinery more complex than ever seen before. To disprove this theory, Kempelen allowed magnets to come close to the box. The Turk still won, so people decided it must be witchcraft after all.

By the time Kempelen and his invention arrived in London, no one had figured out the secret. Now, lowly commoners were able to try their luck against the machine, but still the Turk rarely lost. All the great thinkers of the day felt compelled to write about him, so there were tons of pamphlets and books circulating about the intelligent robot.

Finally, at the end of his two-year touring stint, Kempelen returned home and dismantled the Turk again. He planned on taking the

Creating a Masterpiece

Edgar Allen Poe's poems could depress a puppy, they were so bleak. Before he started down the road to misery, he saw the Turk play in 1835. It inspired him to write an article debunking the mystery of the Turk.

Poe was dead wrong in his article, but that's because he said the same things all the doubters before him had. The article did get Poe quite a bit of attention, though, and it helped him form his deductive skills. The format he used to write about the Turk would be used over and over again in his soon-to-be-famous mysteries like "The Murders in the Rue Morgue" where detectives used deductive skills to find the killer. So, did the Turk help create the first detective story? Maybe.

secret of his invention to the grave. But the Turk, like the Terminator, had other plans.

I'll Be Back

Johann Maelzel and the Turk were meant for each other. Both had panache, and both were good at tricking people. Maelzel knew this, and he tried hard to get Kempelen to realize this as well. Kempelen set a high price though, and Maelzel had to wait until Kempelen died. Luckily for both Maelzel and the Turk, Kempelen's son just wanted to make a few francs and sold the chess-player for half the price his dad had asked.

It didn't take long for Maelzel to rediscover the Turk's secret and to breathe new life into his dusty parts after a twenty-year retirement. If it wasn't for him, the Turk might have stayed in some stuffy Austrian attic for centuries more.

After adding a bit of flair to the Turk, like a voice box that would exclaim, "Echec!" ("Check!" in French), Maelzel also went on a tour of Europe—but he was actually excited about it. Maelzel would finally be able to rub shoulders with the cream of the crop, just like he knew he deserved. Europe would never know what hit 'em.

Napoleon, a notoriously poor loser in everything from games to wars, offered to play the newly refurbished chess-player. There are many differing accounts of the event (as there usually are in history) but in each one, Napoleon tried to cheat multiple times, forcing the Turk to sweep all the pieces off the board. (Some versions claim the chess pieces went flying due to the emperor overturning the table in rage at losing.)

Maelzel was tickled pink. Soon his automaton was the main act in a big show of metal moving parts. Maelzel himself became friends with the likes of Beethoven and French royalty. He had hit the big time. Well, sort of.

At one point, Maelzel had to flee Europe to escape debt collectors. But that ended up being Europe's loss, because Maelzel left the continent, taking the automaton to America with him.

They swept through all the big East Coast American cities, inspiring both love and hatred among the people who faced off with the Turk. Along the way, they also influenced many people—and not just those interested in science.

Let's take this to the battlefield, shall we?

Maelzel came across a young P. T. Barnum during one of the Turk's exhibitions. He gave the kid some advice on how to use the press to attract more customers. Combining mystery, oddities, and showmanship into a spectacle was something at which the young Barnum excelled, being in the circus and all. Maelzel told him he was on the right track toward success, and today, the Ringling Bros. and Barnum and Bailey's circus still draws crowds, calling itself "The Greatest Show on Earth."

Abracadabra!

So how did the Turk actually work? Like most magic tricks, the truth isn't nearly as exciting as the trick. And like most magic, illusion is the key.

Not Just a Pretty Face

Kempelen did more than create the Turk. Once he finally got his way and went back to L.A.T (Life After Turk), he kept inventing things. He created an exploding steam engine (although the exploding part wasn't planned), a typewriter for the blind, and a talking machine.

The talking machine that a young Alexander Graham Bell saw years later was a replica of Kempelen's original. The sight inspired him and he invented his own talking machine. Today, we call it a telephone.

Maelzel also continued inventing, although he died aboard a ship next to the Turk, still deeply in love with it. Before his death, though, he created a portable metronome to keep the beat in music, an orchestrion (picture a robot orchestra), and a panharmonicon—an automaton that played military music.

chess master:

Kempelen figured out it was safer to approach a chess master, let him in on the secret, and have him be the operator than try to play against him, and probably lose.

The Turk wasn't an intelligent, self-thinking automaton. In fact, he wasn't an automaton at all. None of his mechanical clockwork parts moved his body, and he didn't follow a set of predetermined steps. His arms moved by levers put in motion by the operator and he didn't think for himself. The Turk couldn't even tell you the time!

Instead, the elaborate ritual of opening all of the doors and shining a light in the dark cabinet only helped mask what was really happening when the Turk went into action. A person, usually a chess master in on the secret, sat hidden inside the box.

Each time a new door was opened, the hidden **chess master** scooted to the opposite side on an oiled bench. The chess player didn't even have to be child-sized; they just had to know when to bend and roll in order to stay out of sight.

The smoke from the operator's candle went out through the Turk's turban, and air holes were poked into the box. In the days before electricity, rooms were always smoke-filled, so no one noticed a little extra smoke hanging about the Turk like a halo. If the candle went out, the operator had a system worked out to notify Kempelen and, later, Maelzel. The box was still a dark, smoky place to hang out, so the shows were limited to an hour long. You know, so the operator wouldn't pass out. That kind of thing would give the Turk away.

Not everything about the Turk was fake, though. Those levers the Turk relied on to move his arm were quite creative, and there were magnets involved after all. Magnets were placed above the head of the operator inside the box, each one corresponding to a chess piece. When the opponent made a move, the magnets told the hidden chess master which pieces went where. (The magnets

Not the actual inner workings.

Kempelen and Maelzel allowed near the box did nothing to affect the ones inside due to their positioning.)

All of the machinery, creaks, and noises added to the mystique of a working automaton. In the end, people wanted to believe in the mystery, so they did. It wasn't a bad thing, either, since it helped inspire not one, but two revolutions—the Industrial and the computer.

When Lying Is a Good Thing

Okay, so the Turk was a big fat fraud. At least he wasn't taking over the world anytime soon. And even better, the chess-player inspired some real inventions that you would miss today.

While all those skeptics thought no machine could ever be capable of playing chess, another guy thought exactly the opposite. Charles Babbage had always been interested in mechanical objects. So he decided to challenge the Turk. Babbage was convinced that the Turk was a fake, but he thought such a machine was possible. It just needed the right, smart guy to figure it out. And he knew just the smart guy capable of making a robot play chess or checkers—himself.

Babbage got so excited about his own dream to build such a machine that he made himself sick. After a short vacation to help stop the vomiting and hives, he drew up plans for a machine that could think on its own, in a way. Many failures, bankruptcy, and sleepless nights later, Babbage created the forerunner to the modern computer.

It was this desire to imitate life that led to more mechanical developments and more complex machinery. The Industrial Revolution gained steam directly from the popularity of automatons. People started thinking, "Wouldn't it be great if the robot got its hands rubbed raw from weaving instead of mine?" So they came up with cool inventions like the power loom to do all the grunt work.

In fact, the power loom—invented by Edmund Cartwright—was inspired by none other than the Turk himself, allegedly. Cartwright saw the Turk play in London (while it was touring with Kempelen) and thought it was terrific. Sure, he believed an automaton really was playing chess, but it allowed him to think if that was possible, anything was possible. We'll forgive him this mistake, since it led to the power loom three years later and mass-produced clothing today.

Lessons from a Computer

It wasn't until 1997 that a machine finally beat a human chess master. Soviet Garry Kasparov had beat a chess-playing computer called Deep Blue (as well as all those nerds who built him) in 1989 and then again in 1996. Confident he'd keep winning, Kasparov agreed to a third match in 1997. He figured it was his duty to protect the human race from intelligent computers of the chess-playing ilk.

Deeper Blue (the new computer) brought his thinking cap this time—meaning he had his hardware upgraded. This allowed the computer to analyze two hundred million positions per second. The computer won, and Kasparov was stunned. He demanded a rematch, insisting Deeper Blue had cheated, but no dice. The creators quickly retired their creation and refused any more matches. That's how to quit when you're ahead.

Kasparov himself, not the least bit bitter.

Acknowledgments

Like many of the men and women between these pages, this book would have never existed if it weren't for the enthusiasm of many more living and breathing people. Thanks to Carrie Pestritto for never giving up hope and for finding Julie Matysik, the perfect editor; Bethany Stark, for the right dose of illustrative humor; Rita Gartley and Frances Lovato, for always being at the library; Professor Michael Barnes for vetting scholarly books and looking over Homer (any mistakes are mine); my supportive family, and my friends, Jacki Shepherd, Stevie Lloyd, Barbara Krutulis, and Ron Erickson for their insightful contributions.

And mostly, thanks to my husband, Tim Hammerly. He is bigger than life.

Notes on Sources

Chapter One

John Green's highly entertaining YouTube Channel, Crash Course World History, does a great video on "2,000 Years of Chinese History," which had a great segment on Confucius and Tian. A comparison of Confucius's many confusing lives came from the sources as well as a nice summary from Stanford's *Encyclopedia of Philosophy*.

Chapter Two

You can throw a stick and hit about fifty books on George Washington in any given library. They're everywhere. So I stuck with reading all of Ron Chernow's *Washington*, and corroborated his findings with a variety of others.

Chapter Three

Pythagoras was pretty wily in evading detection, but I managed to track down good books on his baloney butt by Alberto A. Martinez and Carl

Huffman. Original sources from ancient philosophers shed light as well as Stanford's *Encyclopedia of Philosophy*.

Chapter Four

Original sources such as speeches and Benjamin Franklin's letters helped on the Iroquois's contribution to the budding United States. The Iroquois Museum and basic biographies helped tell me the legend of Hiawatha. Grinnell College's website clarified the various roles of the *wampum* beads.

Chapter Five

M. L. West's *East Face of Helicon* has a lot of great research on the transmission of oral and written poetry from East to West, and much of the information about Gilgamesh comes from there as well as the various essays in *Blackwell's Companions to the Ancient World*. The Arkansas State Religious Studies website provided a blow-by-blow of the many tablets of the epic. The version you got is a mixture of Standard Version and Old Babylonian version. The definitive scholarship on the Sumerian King List is from 1939—yes that long ago—and was written by Thorkild Jacobsen.

Chapter Six

Ben Macintyre wrote the book on Operation Mincemeat. Literally.

Chapter Seven

Shakespeare was tricky. There are so many passionate people arguing many ways about Shakespeare's existence. I tried to keep my bias to a minimum and referenced both sides of the argument. Stephan Greenblatt wrote his book without acknowledging the controversy, and the Declaration of Reasonable doubt is a great site for all those doubters out there. Information about collaboration in Elizabethan and Jacobean times came from

University of North Carolina at Chapel Hill's Alan C. Dessen and Oxford's Brian Vickers.

Chapter Eight

Pope Joan is highly controversial still. There's over five hundred mentions of her in various libraries around the world, but I tried to look at both sides of the coin—both Catholic and Protestant sources. Anything too fanciful or wishful I avoided like a pope down Vicus Papissa. Thanks again to John Green's *Crash Course Renaissance* video for explaining what humanists focus on!

Chapter Nine

Again, I relied on those scholars who have devoted their lives to figuring out which came first: Homer or *The Iliad*. There are many views on how exactly a performer preformed, and, of course, these things changed over the centuries. I used Dr. Nagy's views, *Blackwell's Companions to the Ancient World* was especially great, and Yale's *Open Courses Introduction to Greek History* by Donald Kagan helped me remember my own days at the University of Missouri in the Classics department. Go Tigers!

Chapter Ten

Don't discount dissertations! Michael E. Brooks did all the grunt work on Prester John in his paper, *Prester John: A Reexamination and Compendium of the Mythical Figure Who Helped Spark European Expansion*.

Chapter Eleven

The legends of the Sage Emperors come from many places including Anne Birrell's *Chinese Mythology*, Keith G. Steven's *Chinese Mythological Gods*, and Cultural China's website. Again, John Green's Crash Course World History, does a great video on "2,000 Years of Chinese History" to keep all those dynasties and their Tian-shaming ways straight. More scholars like Michael Puett and Mark Edward Lewis had great insights on the Warring States Period's elite, and the evolution of Huangdi from oral tradition to modern-day god.

Chapter Twelve

Tom Standage's *The Turk* covers the history of both owners, as well as Deep Blue's showdown in 1989, 1996, and 1997.

Sources

Chapter One

Confucius. *The Analects*. Translated by Raymond Dawson. New York: Oxford University Press, 2008.

Green, John. "2000 Years of Chinese History!" *Crash Course World History*. Podcast video. March 8, 2012. www.youtube.com/watch?v=ylWORyToTo4.

Kelen, Betty. *Confucius: In Life and Legend*. New York: Thomas Neslon, 1971.

Stanford Encyclopedia of Philosophy. Stanford University, Sept. 2006. Jan 2013. http://plato.stanford.edu/entries/confucius/.

Wilker, Josh. *Confucius: Philosopher and Teacher*. New York: Franklin Watts, 1999.

Chapter Two

Carbone, Gerald M. *Washington*. New York: Palgrave Macmillan, 2010.

Chernow, Rob. *Washington: A Life*. New York: Penguin Press, 2010.

George Washington. BrainyQuote.com, Xplore Inc, 2014. www.brainyquote.com/citation/quotes/quotes/g/georgewash135802.html.

George Washington's Mount Vernon. Last modified 2014. www.mountvernon.org/.

Green, John. "Who Won the American Revolution?" *Crash Course US History*. Podcast video. March 14, 2013. www.youtube.com/watch?v=3EiSymR-rKI4&list=PL8dPuuaLjXtMwmepBjTSG593eG7ObzO7s.

Morris Jr., Seymour. *American History Revised: 200 Startling Facts*. New York: Broadway Books, 2010.

PBS. www.pbs.org/opb/historydetectives/feature/british-navy-impressment/.

Woods Jr., Thomas E. 33 *Questions About American History You're Not supposed to Ask*. New York: Crown Forum, 2007.

Chapter Three

Aristotle. *Fragments*. Translated by Jonathan Barnes and Gavin Lawrence. Vol. 2 of *The Complete Works of Aristotle*. Princeton, NJ: Princeton University Press, 1984.

Burkert, Walter. *Lore and Science in Ancient Pythagoreanism*. Cambridge, MA: Harvard University Press, 1972.

Huffman, Carl. "Pythagoras." Stanford Encyclopedia of Philosophy. Last modified August 8, 2011. Accessed October 21, 2013. http://plato.stanford.edu/entries/pythagoras/.

Laertius, Diogenes. *Lives of Eminent Philosophers*. Translated by R. D. Hicks. Cambridge, MA: Harvard University Press, 1925.

Martinez, Alberto A. *The Cult of Pythagoras: Math and Myths*. Pittsburgh, PA: Pittsburgh University Press, 2012.

Zhmud, Leonid. *Pythagoras and the Early Pythagoreans*. Translated by Kevin Windle and Rosh Ireland. Oxford, England: Oxford University Press, 2012.

Chapter Four

"All About Wampum." Grinnell College. Last modified 2001. http://web.grinnell.edu/courses/edu/f01/edu315-01/liberato/wampum.html.

Canassatego. "Excerpts from speeches by Canassatego, an Iroquois, as printed by Benjamin Franklin, 1740s." Smithsonian Source. Last modified 2007. www.smithsoniansource.org/display/primarysource/viewdetails.aspx?PrimarySourceId=1195.

Dennis, Matthew. "The League of the Iroquois." The Gilder Lehrman Institute of American History. Accessed May 23, 2014. www.gilderlehrman. org/history-by-era/american-indians/essays/league-iroquois.

Franklin, Benjamin. "Benjamin Franklin on the Iroquois League, in a letter to James Parker, 1751." Smithsonian Source. Last modified 2007. www.smithsonian-source.org/display/primarysource/viewdetails.aspx?PrimarySourceId=1198.

Green, John. "The Black Legend, Native Americans, and Spaniards" *Crash Course US History*. Podcast video. January 31, 2013. www.youtube. com/watch?v=6E9WU9TGrec&list=PL8dPuuaLjXtMwmepBjTS-G593eG7ObzO7s&index=2.

Iroquois Museum. www.iroquoismuseum.org/.

Johansen, Bruce E. *Forgotten Founders: Benjamin Franklin, the Iroquois, and the Rationale for the American Revolution*. Ipswich, MA: Gambit Inc, 1982.

McCarld, Megan and George Ypsilantis. *Hiawatha and the Iroquois League*. Alvin Josephy's Biography Series of American Indians. Englewood Cliffs, NJ: Silver Burdett Press, 1989.

Morgan, Lewis Henry. *League of the Iroquois*. Seacaucus, NJ: Carol Publishing Group, 1962.

Chapter Five

Foley, John Miles, ed. *A Companion to Ancient Epic*. Blackwell's Companions to the Ancient World. Malden, MA: Blackwell, 2005.

Hooker, Richard. "The Epic of Gilgamesh." Arkansas State. www.clt.astate. edu/.

Jacobsen, Thorkild. *The Sumerian King List*. Assyriological Studies 11. Chicago, IL: The University of Chicago, 1939.

Katz, Dina. "Gilgamesh and Akka: Was Uruk Rule By Two Assemblies?" *Revue d'Assyriologie et d'Archeologie Orientale* 81 (1987): 105–114.

Michigan Department of Education. *Michigan's Genre Project*. Accessed October 22, 2013. http://michigan.gov/documents/mde/Genre_Project_197249_7.pdf.

New Day. "Blueprint for Noah's Ark Found?" CNN. Video file, 4:43. January 28, 2014. www.cnn.com/video/data/2.0/video/bestoftv/2014/01/28/noahs-ark-blueprint-finkel-newday.cnn.html.

West, M. L. *The East Face of Helicon: West Asiatic Elements in Greek Poetry and Myth*. Oxford, New York City: Clarendon Press, 1997.

Chapter Six

Crowdy, Terry. *Deceiving Hitler: Double Cross and Deception in World War II*. London: Osprey Publishing, 2008.
Macintyre, Ben. *Operation Mincemeat*. New York: Broadway Paperbacks, 2010.
Rice, Earle. *Strategic Battles in Europe*. San Diego, CA: Lucent Books, 2000.

Chapter Seven

Declaration of Reasonable Doubt. Last modified 2013. http://doubtabout-will.org/declaration.
Dessen, Alan C. "The Elizabethan and Jacobean Script-to-Stage Process: The Playwright, Theatrical Intentions, and Collaboration." *In Shakespeare and Intention*. Published in *Style* 44 no. 3 (2010): 391–403.
Greaves, Richard L. *Society and Religion in Elizabethan England*. Minneapolis, MN: University of Minnesota, 1981.
Greenblatt, Stephan. *Will in the World: How Shakespeare Became Shakespeare*. New York: W. W. Norton and Company, 2004.
"How We Know that Shakespeare Wrote Shakespeare." http://shakespeareau-thorship.com/howdowe.html.
The Shakespearean Authorship Trust. www.shakespeareanauthorshiptrust.org.uk/.
Vickers, Brian. *Shakespeare, Co-Author: A Historical Study of Five Collaborative Plays*. Oxford, England: Oxford University Press, 2002.

Chapter Eight

Grayson, Saisha. "Disruptive Disguises: The Problem of Transvestite Saints for Medieval Art, Identity, and Identification." In the *Journal of the Society for Medieval Feminist Scholarship*. MFF 45, no.2 (2009): 138–74. http://ir.uiowa.edu/cgi/viewcontent.cgi?article=1814&context=mff.

Kirsch, Johann Peter. "Popess Joan." *The Catholic Encyclopedia*. Vol. 8. New York: Robert Appleton Company, 1910. March 10, 2014. www.newadvent.org/cathen/08407a.htm.

Mystery Files. "Pope Joan." Season 2, Episode 9. Smithsonian Channel. First broadcast June 10, 2011. Directed by Ben Mole.

Pardoe, Rosemary and Darroll. *The Female Pope*. Northhamptonshire, England: Crucible, 1988.

Rustici, Craig M. *The Afterlife of Pope Joan*. Ann Arbor, MI: The University of Ann Arbor Michigan, 2006.

Chapter Nine

Foley, John Miles. ed. *A Companion to Ancient Epic*. Blackwell's Companions to the Ancient World. Malden, MA: Blackwell, 2005.

Kagan, Donald. "Introduction to Ancient Greek History." Lectures presented at Yale, New Haven, CT. Video File. 2007. http://oyc.yale.edu/classics/clcv-205.

Makrinos, Antony. "The Reception of Homer in Byzantium." UCL Lunch Hour Lectures. Video file, 31:53. Dec 8, 2003. Accessed October 4, 2013. www.ucl.ac.uk/lhl/lhlpub_spring09/04_290109.

Martin, Thomas R. "The Nature of the Noble Man for Alexander the Great the 'Man Who Loved Homer.'" *The Center for Hellenic Studies*. Last Modified 2012. http://chs.harvard.edu/wa/pageR¿tn=ArticleWrapper&bdc=12&mn=4358.

Nagy, Gregory. *Greek Mythology and Poetics*. Ithaca, NY: Cornell University Press, 1990.

Nagy, Gregory. "Performance and Text in Ancient Greece." *The Center for Hellenic Studies*. Last Modified 2012. http://chs.harvard.edu/wa/pageR¿tn=ArticleWrapper&bdc=12&mn=3626.

"Papyrus fragment with lines from Homer's Odyssey [Greek, Ptolemaic] (09.182.50)." In *Heilbrunn Timeline of Art History*. New York: The Metropolitan Museum of Art, 2000–.www.metmuseum.org/toah/works-of-art/09.182.50 (April 2007).

West, M. L. *The East Face of Helicon: West Asiatic Elements in Greek Poetry and Myth*. Oxford, New York City: Clarendon Press, 1997.

Wiles, David. *Greek Theatre Performance: An Introduction*. Cambridge: Cambridge University Press, 2000.

Chapter Ten

Bar-Ilan, M. "Prester John: Fiction and History." *History of European Ideas*, 20/1-3 (1995): 291–298. http://shoko.lnx.biu.ac.il/~barilm/presjohn.html.

British Library. Medieval Realms. www.bl.uk/learning/histcitizen/medieval/monsters/medievalmonsters.html.

Brooks, Michael E. "Prester John: A Reexamination and Compendium of the Mythical Figure Who Helped Spark European Expansion." PhD dissertation, University of Toledo, 2009.

Gumilev, Lev. *Searches for an Imaginary Kingdom: The Legend of the Kingdom of Prester John*. Translated by R. E. F. Smith. New York: Cambridge University Press, 1987.

Heng, Geraldine. *An Empire of Magic: Medieval Romance and the Politics of Cultural Fantasy*. New York: Columbia University Press, 2003.

Chapter Eleven

Birrell, Anne. *Chinese Mythology: An Introduction*. Baltimore, MD: The John Hopkins University Press, 1993.

Chang, Chun-Shu. *Nation, State, and Imperialism in Han China*. Vol. 1 of *The Rise of the Chinese Empire*. Ann Arbor, MI: University of Michigan, 2007.

Curran, James. Review of *The Yellow Emperor's Classics of Internal Medicine*. *US National Library of Medicine*. Last Modified April 2005. www.ncbi.nlm.nih.gov/pmc/articles/PMC2287209/.

Green, John. "2,000 Years of Chinese History!" *Crash Course World History*. Podcast video. March 8, 2012. www.youtube.com/watch?v=ylWORy-ToTo4.

Lagerwey, John, and Marc Kalinowski, eds. *Shang Through Han*. Vol. 1 of *Early Chinese Religion*. Boston: Brill Academic Pub, 2009.

Poceski, Mario. *Introducing Chinese Religions*. London: Routledge, 2009.

Puett, Michael. *The Ambivalence of Creation: Debates Concerning Innovation and Artifice in Early China.* Stanford: Stanford University Press, 2001.

Puett, Michael. *To Become a God: Cosmology, Sacrifice, and Self-Divinization in Early China.* Boston: Harvard University Asia Center, 2004.

Stevens, Keith G. *Chinese Mythological Gods.* Oxford: Oxford University Press, 2001.

"The Yellow Emperor." Cultural China. Last modified 2014. http://History.cultural-china.com/en/46History1159.html.

Chapter Twelve

Bedini, Silvio A. "The Role of Automata in the History of Technology." http://xroads.virginia.edu/~drbr/b_edini.html.

Gopnik, Adam. "A Point of View: Chess and 18th Century Artificial Intelligence." March 22, 2013. www.bbc.co.uk/news/magazine-21876120.

Standage, Tom. *The Turk: The Life and Times of the Famous Eighteenth Century Chess Playing Machine.* New York: Walker and Company, 2002.

Wood, Gaby. *Edison's Eve: A Magical History of the Quest for Mechanical Life.* New York: Alfred A. Knopf, 2002.

Image Credits

Chapter One

Confucius temple and statue (Thinkstock # 177703619; photographer: OSTILL)

Analects by Confucius and followers in 2nd century BCE, courtesy of Wikimedia Commons Public Domain / Source: http://kanbun.info/keibu/rongo0307.html via Fukutaro in 2007

Famous Confucian Statue of the Ashikaga Gakko, courtesy of Wikimedia Commons Public Domain / Source: Abasaa in 2013

Chapter Two

Image of dentures courtesy of Mount Vernon Ladies' Association

George Washington on a horse at age 45 courtesy of Mount Vernon Ladies' Association

George Washington the First Good President started by Gilbert Stuart in 1797, finished in 1846, courtesy of Wikimedia Commons Public Domain / Source: Clark Art Institute via Docu 2010

John Hancock signature, courtesy of Wikimedia Commons Pubic Domain / Source: US Declaration of Independence via Tim Packer 2006

Grand Union Flag, courtesy of Wikimedia Commons Public Domain / Source: Hosie 2006

Chapter Three

Pythagoras teaching (Thinkstock # 92846197; photographer: Photos.com)
Woodcut of Pythagorean Harmonies by Franchino Gaffurio in 1490, courtesy of Wikimedia Commons Public Domain / Source: www.chmtl.indiana.edu/tml/15th/GAFTM1_02GF.gif via Zupftom in 2009

Chapter Four

Hiawatha's Belt courtesy of the Iroquois Indian Museum
Map of the early United States courtesy of the University of Texas Libraries
An Iroquois longhouse, courtesy of Wikimedia Commons Public Domain / Source: Gordy, Wilbur F. Stories of American History. New York: Charles Scribner's Sons, 1920. Page 20.

Chapter Five

Gilgamesh Flood tablet (Thinkstock # 92819125; photographer: Photos.com)
Ziggurat of Ur, courtesy of Wikimedia Commons / Public Domain by author Tla2006 / photograph taken July 1, 2006
Meso map, courtesy of Wikimedia Commons / CC BY-SA 2.5 by author Joeyhewitt in 2012

Chapter Six

Major Martin ID card from 1943 photograph taken in 1953, courtesy of Wikimedia Commons Public Domain / Source: Ewen Montagu team via Belissarius in 2011
Operation Husky Principal Targets Map, courtesy of Wikimedia Commons Public Domain / Source: The Army Air Forces in WWII, Volume 2 via 489thCorsica in 2009

Chapter Seven

Shakespeare's Six Known Signatures, courtesy of Wikimedia Commons Public Domain / Two Sources: *Shakespeare and his Times*, and *Shakespeare's Handwriting* via Tom Reedy in 2011
Shakespeare's home (Thinkstock # 89208375)

Chapter Eight

Pope Joan from a tarot card deck 1450, courtesy of Wikimedia Commons Public Domain / Source: Pierpont Morgan Library via Shakko in 2009

Chapter Nine

Homer Statue with Lyre (Thinkstock # 94210907; photographer: Gregory Markov)
Odeon of Herodes Atticus (Thinkstock #176990598; photographer: Nils Prause)

Chapter Ten

Prester John map by Ortelius in 1603, courtesy of Wikimedia Commons Public Domain / Source: Theatrum obis terrarium via Woudloper 2007
Illustration from the Nuremburg Chronicle by Hartmann Schedel 1493, courtesy of Wikimedia Commons Public Domain / Source: Beloit College via Chris 73 in 2006
Christopher Columbus's copy of Marco Polo's *Travels* 15th century, courtesy of Wikimedia Commons Public Domain / Source: "Le Livre des Merveilles" via World Imaging in 2007
Battle between Mongols and Chinese in 1211 (1430), courtesy of Wikimedia Commons Public Domain / Source: Bibliotheque nationale de France, Department des Manuscrits, Divisions orientale via Bahatur 2010
Crusader art (Thinkstock #92831883; photographer: Photos.com)

Chapter Eleven

Chi You, courtesy of Wikimedia Commons Public Domain / Source: http://www1.vecceed.ne.jp/~watagi/page022.html via 2006
Mausoleum of Huangdi image courtesy of C. B. Wentworth
Footprints of Huangdi image courtesy of C. B. Wentworth
CMOC Treasures of Ancient China Exhibit Dagger-Axe, courtesy of Wikimedia Commons / CC BY-SA 2.5 by author Editor at Large in 2007
Great Wall and Terracotta figure (Thinkstock #175564737; photographer Hung_Chung_Chih)
Five Races Flag, courtesy of Wikimedia Commons Public Domain / Source: Eric-metro 2012

Chapter Twelve

Garry Kasparov playing chess (Thinkstock # 2707888; photographer Mario Tama)
Photo of the Reconstruction of the Chess Playing Automaton, courtesy of Wikimedia Commons CC-BY-SA-3.0,2.5,2.0,1.0 / Attribution: Carafe at en.wikipedia 2007
Automaton in the Swiss Museum CIMA 8332, courtesy of Wikmedia Commons CeCill / Attribution: Marku 1988 in 2007
Joseph Racknitz's The Turk, courtesy of Wikimedia Commons Public Domain / Source: Humbolt University pilot natural history project: Die Wissenschaftlichen Sammlungen

Index